The Big Book of Slots Slots Slots and Video Poker

The Big Book of

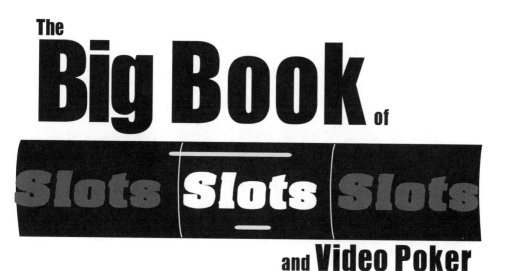

Slots Slots Slots

and Video Poker

Marten Jensen

CARDOZA PUBLISHING

Cardoza Publishing is the foremost gaming and gambling publisher in the world with a library of more than 200 up-to-date and easy-to-read books and strategies. These authoritative works are written by the top experts in their fields and with more than 10,000,000 books in print, represent the best-selling and most popular gaming books anywhere.

SECOND EDITION

Copyright© 2006, 2010 by Marten Jensen
-All Rights Reserved-

Library of Congress Catalog Card No: 2009937735
ISBN 13: 978-1-58042-239-0
ISBN 10: 1-58042-239-X

CONTENTS

CHAPTER 2: SLOT MACHINE ELEMENTS 29

CHAPTER 3: MONEY MATTERS 39

TABLE OF CONTENTS

TABLE OF CONTENTS

GLOSSARY   271

INTRODUCTION

Not long ago, there was little point to reading a book on slot machines—if you could even find such a book. The machines were all very similar: they each had three reels, a coin slot, a coin tray at the bottom, and an arm at the right side. You just dropped in a coin and pulled down the arm. The reels spun around, and if you were lucky, you won a few coins.

Over the past ten to fifteen years, however, slot machine technology has undergone a major revolution. Many machines today have become a kind of computer game and have little resemblance to the old mechanical contraptions of twenty or more years ago. Yet other than pushing a button instead of pulling a lever, most slot players have not changed their playing style.

Typically, today's players still enter the casino with a few hundred dollars in their pockets, plop down at any unoccupied machine, and begin to spin the reels. When they eventually run out of gambling money, they go see a show or just go home. If they do get lucky and win a jackpot, they keep on playing until they have given all their winnings back to the casino. They never expected to come out ahead, anyway. That is the sum total of their casino experience.

DID YOU KNOW...?

For a long, long time, all slot machines had three mechanical spinning reels, a single payline, and no player choices. Today, most new slot games have a video screen with five or more simulated reels, multiple paylines, multiple credit wagers, and plenty of choices. This means you now have to learn the right way to play each game.

Modern slot machines are no longer the mindless one-armed bandits of yesteryear. Now they are all sophisticated electronic devices, although the ones with actual mechanical spinning reels do try to hide the fact that they are fully controlled by the latest computer technology. So how does this affect you, the average player? If you are not completely familiar with the game you are playing, and if you are not playing the best way possible, you will likely lose your money at a faster rate than the designed-in payback would indicate.

WHY READ THIS BOOK?

So how do you avoid falling into this trap? That's simple! Just read this book. In fact, there are ways to actually beat certain slot games, and this book will show you how to do it. You will learn how to maximize your chances of winning on every different kind of slot machine in the casinos. You will know how to find the best machines to play and how to play them to win. This book will even tell you how to find and play games in which you have a better than even chance of winning the money.

Fifty years ago, a few slot machines were tucked away in the corners of the casinos and in back hallways. Today, electronic gaming devices—an industry term that includes slots, video poker, video keno, etc.—are everywhere and account for almost three-quarters of the total revenues in all American casinos. Considering the huge popularity of slot machines, it is somewhat curious that there are still relatively few good books on the subject. The intent of this book is to fill that void.

REEL GOOD ADVICE

If you don't have time to read this entire book before starting to play, jump over to Chapter 9, where you'll be given some simple advice to get you going. You can always read about the advanced strategy when you have more time.

Should you play the reel spinners or the video machines, or should you stick with the progressives? This book will fully describe the features of every type of game and how to play it in the most effective manner. I will also show you how to find the loosest slots and how to test a machine to see if it is hot. Do you know the difference between a multiplier, a line game, an option-buy game, and a banking game? If you don't, you will certainly go through your gambling stake very quickly. I will advise you on the best way to play every one of those games, and which ones are the money makers.

Just by thumbing through this book you can see that it is brimming with useful information about every kind of slot machine. When you decide to read the details more carefully, you will learn how to extend your bankroll and how to legitimately overcome the casino's mathematical advantage on some games. These are things that couldn't be done on the old machines—at least not without cheating.

IMPORTANT DECISIONS

Most people think that, unlike video poker players, slot players don't have to make any decisions—they just drop in coins and hit the SPIN button. Wrong! Slot players have plenty of decisions to make, and if they make wrong decisions, or arbitrary ones, they will rarely come out ahead. So what are these important decisions?

The first and most important decision is the selection of the right machine. But aren't they all basically the same? Absolutely not! There is such a variety of slot machines in the casinos, made by numerous competing manufacturers, that some of them are bound to be better than others. The trick is to know how to tell the good from the bad. This book will give you useful guidance in that regard.

Once a suitable game is selected, your second decision is to determine how many coins or credits to wager on each spin. Today, there is no such device as a single-coin slot machine. All modern machines take multiple coins, and the misguided advice to always bet the maximum can cause serious damage to your wallet. You need to know which games are best played with a minimum wager and which always require the maximum. Do it wrong and you will reduce your chances of winning. I will tell you which machine is which.

But things get even more complicated. How do you play a game designed to accept ninety or more credits at a time? Do you really want to play a nickel machine and invest as much as $4.50 on a single spin? I tell you how to tackle that and similar situations.

Slot machine manufacturers are always trying to invent new ways to encourage people to keep on paying and playing. In their enthusiasm, these companies have devised a class of machines called banking games, in which points or some type of assets are accumulated and finally paid out as a big bonus. Knowledgeable players have discovered that these games often reach a point when they are profitable to play. You may find it hard to believe that some slot machines in the casinos are actually beatable. Believe it! I will give you specific suggestions on how to locate these machines and how to win the bonus.

As you read this book, you will learn details on many related topics, such as advice on finding the loosest machines, the advantages of joining slot clubs, and the safest ways to deal with the IRS.

All the ringing bells, flashing lights, and clattering coins tend to mesmerize the majority of slot players. They sit at a machine and spin the reels as fast as they can, hoping they will win one of those big jackpots that they perceive are being won all around them. They believe that if they keep feeding the machine and keep those reels spinning, sooner or later they will also be big winners. And then they wonder why they keep on losing. It's because they really don't know what they're doing!

Once you have read and absorbed this book, you will look at those players and chuckle. They think slot machines are mindless games requiring no particular strategy and that some people are just luckier than others. But you will know better. You will know that by learning about the games and by using a methodical approach, you are much more likely to come out ahead than those poor, unenlightened amateurs.

A LITTLE HISTORY

The spinning reel slot machine was invented over one hundred years ago by August Fey, a German machinist who had immigrated to San Francisco. His invention was called the Liberty Bell, which was a three-reel device in a metal box that contained symbols such as bells, stars, and horseshoes. The top prize was paid when three bells appeared in the window, and it was popularly called a Bell machine. That name stuck for a long time, being generically applied to any slot machine.

Fey's machines soon became very popular, and in 1907, an enterprising fellow in Chicago by the name of Herbert Mills copied Fey's mechanism and started manufacturing slot machines on a large-scale basis. Mills modified Fey's design, however, in that his machine had twenty symbols per reel instead of ten. He also widened the window so the player could now see three rows of symbols, but only the row under the centerline paid anything. Being able to see winning symbols that just missed the payline encouraged many people to keep playing with the thought that they might hit it big on the next pull. This teaser-window design soon became a standard feature in all slot machines.

The Mills Novelty Company was very successful and by the late 1920s had more than one thousand employees. During Prohibition, slot machines evolved into full-fledged gambling devices and rows of them could be found in every speakeasy. By that time, slot machine manufacturing had become a big business, drawing in other competitors, but Mills remained the leader.

Before long, Mills's slot machines were being distributed throughout the country and were installed mostly in saloons and pool halls. In 1912, Nevada legalized slot machines as a form of vending machine, so long as they did not pay out cash awards. During this period, slot machines paid winners with chewing gum and other products. The reels carried pictures of various fruits that represented the different flavors of gum. Many of these symbols are still in use today.

The popular Mills Blue Bell, circa 1949.

By the early 1930s, most slot machine installations were controlled by the mob. When Mayor Fiorello LaGuardia ran the slots out of New York City, the mob took them to New Orleans by invitation of Governor Huey Long, who made millions in kickbacks. Machines controlled by the mob had such a poor payback (typically about 50 percent) that they became known as "one-armed bandits."

INTRODUCTION

Meanwhile, after Nevada legalized gambling in 1931, the first legal casinos installed slot machines for the purpose of distracting and entertaining wives and girlfriends, while the serious gamblers played at the gaming tables. By the time the Flamingo Hotel opened in 1947, many casinos began to view slots as a profit center and improved the payouts to attract more business. This enticed some of the serious gamblers to the slots and began a long-term escalation in the popularity of slot machines in gambling casinos.

All the early slot machines were purely mechanical devices, the internal mechanism consisting of wheels, gears, levers, springs, and cams. In 1931, the Jennings Company developed the first electromechanical slot machine with motor-driven reels. It was not very successful because at that time, many gamblers were wary of such new-fangled technology.

Further improvements were minimal until the 1960s when Bally Manufacturing Company (now named Bally Gaming Systems), a major supplier of pinball machines, entered the market with newly designed electromechanical slots. Soon Bally was introducing machines with multiple coin acceptors and motor-driven coin hoppers that were capable of making much larger and faster payouts. These machines were so successful that by the 1970s, Bally controlled 90 percent of the slot machine market.

In 1975, the development of the first all-electronic video slot machine by the Fortune Coin Company constituted a major departure from the traditional electromechanical machine. In 1978, the Sircoma Company, later renamed International Game Technology (IGT), bought out Fortune Coin, and the product line was soon expanded to include four-reel video slot machines. Although slot machines with video screens were not that much different than their mechanical cousins, they ultimately led to the introduction of video blackjack machines, quickly followed by video poker machines.

IGT had bet its future on the video concept and soon became the leader in video games of all kinds. The versatility and proliferation of video poker and video slot machines ultimately resulted in IGT supplanting Bally as the market leader. Today IGT is the industry powerhouse, although Bally is working hard to make a comeback.

It is interesting to note that over the years the original concept of the slot machine has not significantly changed. Many of today's slots still have three vertical reels with various symbols and an operating arm at the right side (although the arm is rapidly disappearing). Modern machines use credits instead of coins, accept bills of all denominations, and may even have more than three reels, while the purely electronic games simulate spinning reels on video screens—but the basic form remains the same.

SLOT MACHINE OVERVIEW

For a long time, a slot machine consisted of three side-by-side reels that displayed pictures of bells, bars, sevens, and various fruits such as cherries, lemons, and plums. The action was entirely mechanical. After inserting a coin, the reels were set in motion by pulling down a long handle at the right side. The machine paid off by dropping coins into a tray when certain symbols lined up in the window behind the horizontal payline.

Those old mechanical slot machines are now considered to be antiques. Although modern slot machines still use the basic principle of spinning reels with symbols on them, they have become very sophisticated computer-controlled devices. Instead of pulling a handle, which is still an option on some machines, most players activate the reels by pushing a button. Today, almost all slots take multiple coins and have built-in paper currency validators that accept any denomination from $1 to $100. In some of the newest machines, there are as many as six simulated spinning reels displayed on a video screen, using a large variety of symbols.

SLOT MACHINE FAMILIES

Since the 1980s, when the first video and computer-controlled slot machines appeared in casinos, the number of different types and styles of machines has virtually exploded. To get a better understanding of the seemingly endless variety of slots on the casino floors today, I will begin by organizing them into the following families.

Spinning Reel Machines

Although these machines have actual mechanical spinning reels, the final position of the reels is completely computer controlled. Specific strategies for playing reel spinners are covered in a later chapter. Following are the major kinds:

MULTIPLIER GAME

The payout is multiplied by the number of coins or credits wagered.

MULTI-LINE GAME

Additional paylines can be activated by wagering more coins or credits.

OPTION-BUY GAME

Additional winning symbol combinations are activated by betting the maximum number of coins or credits.

BANKING GAME

Points or some form of assets are accumulated in a "bank" and eventually paid out as credits.

Video Machines

These are the newest generation of machines where the spinning reels are simulated on a video screen. The playing strategies for most video games are quite different than for reel spinners and are covered in a separate chapter. The major kinds are:

BONUS GAME

Certain symbol combinations cause a bonus mode to appear on a secondary screen.

BANKING GAME

Points or some form of assets are accumulated in a "bank" and eventually paid out as credits.

MULTI-GAME

The player has a choice of several different games on a single machine.

Progressive Slots

These slots have a dynamic top jackpot that grows larger by pooling a fraction of each wager as the games are played. Groups of machines are usually linked together, all contributing to the same progressive jackpot. Progressive playing strategy is significantly different than the strategies used for reel spinners or video games, and is therefore covered in its own chapter. The major kinds of progressive machines are:

STAND-ALONE PROGRESSIVE

A solitary progressive slot machine that is not linked to any other machine.

LOCAL PROGRESSIVE

One of a bank or carousel of similar progressive machines that are linked together within a single casino.

WIDE AREA PROGRESSIVE SLOT (WAPS)

One of a large number of similar progressive machines that are linked together over a wide geographic area such as a city or a state.

CABINET STYLES

When you look at the different slot machines in a casino, you will note that they come in a variety of cabinet configurations. To reduce the confusion, I've boiled them all down to the following three basic styles:

Upright

This is a vertical cabinet that can easily be played while standing or sitting. It often comes with a backless stool. In the nicer casinos, the stool will have a back, but it's still not a very comfortable place to sit for a long period of time. It may or may not have a pull-arm on the right side, and the coin tray is at the bottom. The cabinet appearance can vary in that it may have a sloped or a domed top, but these are just nonfunctional style features. This is a popular cabinet with the casinos because it uses a minimum amount of floor space.

Slope Front

This is a low-profile cabinet, allowing the player to be comfortably seated in a normal-height chair. It has a sloped horizontal playing surface on which the buttons and the reels (or video screen) are located. The coin slot, bill acceptor, and coin tray are all grouped together at the right side of the playing surface. This cabinet style never includes a pull-arm, allowing the cabinets to be abutted next to each other. In some machines, the rear structure can be rather tall because of a top box with additional game features.

Table Top or Bar Top

These are the video units that are built into a bar top. Like the slope front, the coin slot, bill acceptor, and coin tray are all to the right of the video screen. The seat, of course, is a barstool.

THE MANUFACTURERS

As recently as thirty years ago, there were very few slot machine manufacturers. At that time, Bally was the big gun with 90 percent of the market. Today, there are more than a dozen companies competing for floor space in casinos around the world. Following is a list of the most important slot machine manufacturers:

AC Coin & Slot

Based in Pleasantville, New Jersey, AC Coin & Slot was founded in 1978, about the time gaming was approved in New Jersey. Besides marketing its own games, AC Coin is the exclusive distributor of IGT games in Atlantic City. Its two hottest games: "Triple Stars Slotto" and "King of the Grill" were developed in conjunction with IGT.

Aristocrat Technologies

A major player in Australia since the 1950s, Aristocrat jumped into the European market in the 1960s, but didn't get licensed in Nevada until 2000. Since then, this innovative company has successfully penetrated the U.S. market with video games that have second-screen bonuses and scatter pays, such as "Chicken," "Jumpin' Joey," and "Tropical Delight."

Atronic Americas

Started in 1994, Atronic, which is headquartered in Germany, is now the third largest slot maker in the world. The company is best known for the game "Sphinx," which has been around for five years. Its main platform is the Cashline series that includes games such as "Ghost Hunter," "Sign of Zodiac," and "Mystery."

Bally Gaming Systems

Bally is the oldest of the current crop of slot manufacturers, and can be credited with a number of firsts. In the early 1960s, it successfully marketed an electromechanical machine, followed by the first multicoin slot and the first video multigame slot, the "Game Maker." Before getting into the slot machine business, Bally was a major supplier of arcade games and pinball machines. Its hottest progressive games are the Betty Boop series. Other popular Bally games are "Black & White Double Jackpot," "Blazing 7s," "Stars & Bars," and "Wild Rose."

IGT

IGT's first big success was the Fortune Model 701 Draw Poker machine, which was introduced in 1979. This product started the phenomenal growth of video poker popularity. Then, in 1986, IGT originated the concept of wide-area progressive slots when they convinced a number of casinos in Nevada to install the "Megabucks" machines. These machines, and their offspring, were so successful that today IGT is the largest slot machine manufacturer in the world. It continues to be the leader in the wide-area progressive field with "Megabucks," "Quartermania," "Wheel of Fortune," and "Jeopardy," to name a few. IGT's most popular reel spinners include "Double

Diamond," "Triple Diamond," "Double Diamond Deluxe," "Red, White & Blue," "Sizzling 7s," and many others. "Game King," which is its multigame video slot, has also done quite well.

Konami Gaming

The gaming division of a Japanese company that has been around since 1973, Konami introduced its slots in the United States only three years ago. The company, which is licensed in Nevada as well as in several Tribal jurisdictions, features video-based games such as "All That Glitters" and "Show Me The Mummy."

Mikohn Gaming

Mikohn, a Las Vegas company, has been marketing slot machines for about ten years. For the most part, this company develops and markets games for IGT, the most popular of which are "Clue," "Ripley's Believe It or Not," and the "Yahtzee" series.

WMS Gaming

"Reel 'Em In," which was the first video game with a secondary bonus screen, is still a very popular WMS game. Another innovation, "Piggy Bankin'," was the first banking game to hit the casino floors. Although its clever banking concept was quickly copied by other manufacturers, WMS continued to attract players with "Boom," "Filthy Rich," and the popular "Monopoly" series.

For details on slot machines manufactured by most of the above companies, see Chapter 20.

SLOT MACHINE ELEMENTS

To fully understand how a slot machine works, it is helpful to know the functions of its various components. Although in times past, slot machines consisted of little more than a coin slot and an actuating handle at the right side, today they are far more complex with many buttons, displays, and symbols. The purposes and uses of the major elements found in modern machines are explained in this chapter.

THE PAYTABLE

Every spinning reel machine has the payouts for the winning symbol combinations shown on a posted paytable (also known as the glass). The table is usually located on a panel above the reels and, in some cases, is so extensive that a portion of it is below the reels. It is very important to study the table carefully before starting to play. Among other things, it will tell you if the machine is a multiplier or an option-buy, which is very important information to know. The paytable also provides the information you need to decide if you should play maximum coins or if you can reasonably play one coin at a time. More on this later.

On most video machines you have to press a button to bring the paytable to the screen. This button may be marked PAYTABLE or SEE PAYS. With their bonus and banking features, video paytables can be quite extensive, and it is always worthwhile to study them.

REELS, SYMBOLS, AND PAYLINES

As the name implies, spinning reel slot machines contain spinning reels. These are side-by-side rotating wheels with pictures of various symbols on the outside rims. A small section of the reels may be viewed through a window, which usually displays about three rows of symbols. In modern slots, there are hundreds of different symbols—just about anything the machine designers can dream up.

Across the center of the window is a horizontal line called a payline (see illustration). If a winning symbol combination falls directly under the payline, a payoff occurs. The position of a reel when it comes to rest is called a stop. A reel may stop when a symbol is under the payline or when the blank space between two symbols falls under the payline. A blank space is equivalent to a symbol, and some games actually provide a minor payout for three blank spaces. The symbols just below or just above the payline do not count, unless otherwise stated on the payout display.

Slot window with a single payline.

In video machines, spinning reels are simulated on a video screen. Some video machines mimic the popular three-reel spinners, while many others display five or more simulated reels and three or four rows of symbols. Such machines always have multiple paylines, and the blank spaces have been eliminated.

Whether the reels are mechanical or simulated on a video screen, almost all of today's machines are under the full control of built-in microprocessors and random number generators. More on that later.

SPECIAL SYMBOLS

Considering the proliferation of new symbols in modern slot machines, it is nothing short of amazing that many of the symbols used fifty to one hundred years ago can still be found on some of the most popular machines. In any casino, a quick look around at the various slot paytables will disclose plenty of bells, 7s, and cherries, all of which are historic symbols dating back to the early days of the twentieth century. Lately, however, slot manufacturers have come up with some new twists, which are described below.

Substitute (Wild) Symbols

Since we can have wild cards in a poker game, then we should be able to have wild symbols in a slot machine. Many machines now contain symbols that substitute for any other symbol on the reels, thus they are called substitute symbols. These wild symbols can combine with other symbols to produce a winning combination. For example, 7-7-Wild will give the same payout as 7-7-7.

Multiplier Symbols

As you are examining the payout schedules, searching for that perfect machine, you might enjoy playing one that pays double, triple, or more for certain payline combinations. Such machines have a doubling or tripling substitute (wild) symbol that will multiply the payout for any winning combination. Two doubling symbols on the same payline will quadruple the payout, and two tripling symbols on the same payline will multiply the payout by nine! In addition to multiplying the payout, these symbols act as wild cards in that they automatically become any other symbol to create a winning combination. Most of these are IGT machines. The most popular are Double Diamond and Triple Diamond.

DID YOU KNOW...?

"Five Times Pay" and "Ten Times Pay" are machines with 5x and 10x multipliers. These multipliers operate on the same principle as doubling symbols. For example, if two 10x symbols appear on the same payline, the amount of the payout is multiplied by 100!

Nudge Symbols

How many times have you been rankled because a payoff symbol appeared just above or below the payline? You probably can't count the times when the reels came to rest with two bars on the payline and the third bar just one stop above or below the payline. Exasperating, isn't it?

Not missing a bet, some machines now have certain symbols that are nudged to the payline after the reels stop spinning. The best example is "Double Diamond Deluxe," which is a three-reel machine with Diamond-Bar nudge symbols. When the reels stop and a Diamond-Bar appears just above or below the payline, that reel will move one stop up or down, depending on which way the point of the diamond is facing. Since the diamond is superimposed over one, two, or three bars, this nudge symbol will complete a row of bars. Another example is the "Balloon Bars" game, in which a hot air balloon will float up to the payline if it landed one stop below.

REEL GOOD ADVICE

Keep in mind that nudge symbols are just a psychological gimmick. You may think you are getting a second chance, but the internal microprocessor had already determined the final position of the reels before they even started spinning.

Scatter Symbols

When certain symbols appear anywhere on the screen of a video game, a payout can occur. These scatter symbols do not have to be lined up on any payline, but there usually needs to be at least three of them showing.

Spin Till Win Symbols

When this symbol appears on a payline, the reels will respin by themselves and keep respinning until they stop on a winning combination. Which winning combination you end up with is an entirely random process.

Repeat the Win

Although there is no particular symbol involved, some machines will sometimes respin the reels after a win to repeat that win. Whether or not this occurs is supposed to be randomly determined.

Any Bar (on Paytable)

Many machines have single-, double-, and triple-bar symbols with separate payouts for each type. The Any Bar designation on the paytable means that, on a three-reel machine, you get a payoff for any mix of three bar symbols, regardless of type.

Any Symbol (on Paytable)

This is similar to the Any Bar designation on the paytable, except that you will win with any mix of symbols, so long as there is no blank under the payline.

PLAY BUTTONS

Nearly all of the functions of a slot machine are initiated by electrical pushbutton switches that are activated by a player. In most video games, the functions also appear on the video screen and may be activated by touching the screen. The most common buttons on reel spinners and video games are:

Play buttons on a nine-payline game.

Bet One

On a spinning-reel machine, pressing this button will register as a one-credit bet. It is exactly the same as if you put one coin into the slot, which is an alternative. If you press the button a second time, it will register as a two-credit wager. If you press it a third time, you bet three credits, and so forth. On some machines, this button is marked BET 1 CREDIT.

Play 1 Line, Play 3 Lines, etc.

This row of buttons is found on five-reel video games and typically gives you a choice of one payline, three lines, five lines, seven lines, or nine lines. If you don't press any button, some machines default to the maximum number of paylines.

Bet 1 Per Line, Bet 2 Per Line, etc.

After selecting the number of paylines on a video game, you have to decide how many credits per line you want to bet. The usual choice is one through five, although on some games you can bet as many as ten credits per line. This type of machine usually does not have a SPIN button, so pressing the BET PER LINE button activates the reels.

Bet Max

Pressing this button causes two actions to occur. First, it registers a maximum credit bet, whatever it might be for that machine. If it is a two-coin machine, it will register two coins; if it is a three-coin machine, it will register three coins and so forth. Second, it automatically spins the reels; you don't have to press the SPIN button. On some machines, this button is marked PLAY MAX CREDITS.

Rebet

Pressing this button spins the reels, repeating the exact wager you made on the previous spin.

Spin

After indicating the number of credits you wish to bet or after inserting one or more coins, pressing this button starts the game by causing the reels to spin. If you did not wager any coins or credits, the button will do nothing. On some machines, this button is marked SPIN REELS.

DID YOU KNOW...?

A few machines still have a pull-handle at the right side. Pulling this handle does exactly the same as pressing the SPIN button; in fact, it simply activates an electrical switch that is wired in parallel with the switch under the SPIN button. In times past, when machines had only a pull-handle and no SPIN button, the average rate of play was two hundred to two hundred fifty spins per hour. Today, with almost everyone using the buttons, the average rate of play has gone up to over four hundred spins per hour..

Help

Most video games have a HELP button that brings up a screen with information for novice players, such as the purpose of the various buttons, the configuration of the paylines, and what to do if something malfunctions.

Paytable

Pressing this button on a video game brings the paytable to the screen. It is often several pages in length. Sometimes this button is marked SEE PAYS.

Cash Out

Pressing this button converts any credits accumulated in the machine to coins that are noisily dumped into the metal coin tray. You would normally do this whenever you are ready to leave that machine or any time you want to convert your credits into coins. If a large number of credits is involved, pressing the CASH OUT button may result in the appearance of an attendant who will pay you by hand. More and more machines use cash tickets, which means you will receive a ticket instead of coins. The ticket can be converted to currency by any cashier at that casino. This button is sometimes marked CASH/CREDIT or COLLECT.

Change

Pressing this button illuminates the service light on top of the machine, summoning the change person. Besides calling for change, you should also press the button any time something seems to go wrong with the machine. This button is often marked SERVICE.

DISPLAYS

There are several displays to help the player keep track of bets, credits, and amounts won. There may be some location and terminology variations between different types of machines, but they all perform the same basic functions.

Coin In

This indicator shows how many coins or credits you have committed on the next spin. On some machines, it may be labeled BET or COINS PLAYED. Somewhere on most machines is a sign that states: Pays Only on Coins Accepted. So, before you hit the SPIN button, be sure that the machine accepted as many coins as you intended to bet.

Lines Bet

This indicator shows how many paylines are currently activated, based on which PLAY LINES button you pressed.

Bet Per Line

This indicator shows how many credits you intend to wager on each payline, depending on which BET PER LINE button you pressed.

Total Bet

This is the total amount of your intended wager, which is the number of activated paylines multiplied by the number of credits per payline.

Credits

This keeps track of the amount of credits you have accumulated in the machine. The denomination of each credit is the same as the game denomination; that is, if you are playing a quarter machine, each credit is worth a quarter. The total number of credits goes up whenever you slide a bill into the currency acceptor. On a quarter machine, for example, a ten-dollar bill will add forty credits to the total. The total number of credits also goes up when the machine pays off a winning combination. On the other hand, when you press the BET ONE or MAX BET button, the appropriate number of credits is deducted from the total.

Win Paid

Whenever you win, the amount of the payout is shown on this indicator. This amount is also added to the total in the CREDITS indicator. On some machines, this display is labeled PAID or WINNER PAID.

Insert Coin

This message is illuminated whenever the machine is idle with no bets registered. It turns off when a coin is dropped in or a credit is bet.

Coin Accepted

When you drop in a coin, this message lights up to tell you that the machine is ready for a spin. Of course, the message will not illuminate if the coin is rejected and drops through to the coin tray.

MONEY MATTERS

As we all know, slot machines are driven by money—you risk it and the casino hopes to keep it. Not very long ago, the only money needed to activate any gaming device consisted solely of coins. Today the money takes on several different forms, including paper currency, credits, tokens, and cash tickets. Coins, in fact, are becoming one of the less important kinds of money used in modern slot machines.

DENOMINATIONS

The denomination of a slot machine is defined as the smallest amount of money needed to spin the reels. The casinos and the slot manufacturers have taken this about as far as possible, in that there are machines in all the following denominations on the casino floors:

1¢, 2¢, 5¢, 10¢, 25¢, 50¢, $1, $2, $5, $10, $25, $50, $100, and $500

If you have an odd coin or bill burning a hole in your pocket, the casinos want to be sure you have a place to spend it.

Yes, there are plenty of penny slot machines out there. The new ones accept paper money and allow you to bet up to one thousand coins ($10), so they are quite profitable for the casinos. Because the penny machines used to be very tight, the old advice was not to play them. That advice is no longer valid.

At the other end of the spectrum are the $100 and $500 machines. If you haven't seen one of these, just step into the high-limit slot area of the classiest casinos. For ordinary people, however, the majority of the machines accept nickels, quarters, or dollars—nickels and quarters being the most popular denomination in most venues.

SLOT TALK

A group of machines arranged in a circle or an oval is called a carousel. For your convenience, a change person is usually stationed in the center. A group of machines lined up against a wall or back-to-back is called a bank of slots.

As you search through the casino aisles looking for games in your favorite denomination, pay attention to the lights on top of the machines, known as candles or service lights. They are color-coded according to denomination, which can be helpful in locating your favorite games. If you forget the codes, you can easily refresh your memory by looking at the different machines when you get to the casino.

DID YOU KNOW...?

The service lights on top of slot machines are color-coded by denomination as follows:

WHITE	=	penny
RED	=	nickel
GREEN	=	dime
YELLOW	=	quarter
ORANGE or GOLD	=	half dollar
BLUE	=	one dollar
PURPLE	=	five dollar.

When most slot machines began accepting paper money and registering credits, it was inevitable that multidenominational machines would be the next step. And, sure enough, they have arrived. Typically, they offer a choice of 5¢, 25¢, or $1, or a similar combination. All the player has to do is insert a bill and then push a button indicating the denomination choice. After that, the machine plays like any other.

COINS, BILLS, AND CREDITS

Not very long ago, almost all slot machines accepted only coins and paid out jackpots by dumping coins into the metal coin tray with a loud clatter. Then came the credit machines that converted coins to credits and paid out winnings by running up more credits on the credit meter. The only time you would hear the clatter of coins was when someone pushed the CASH OUT button. Today, almost all machines accept bills and register the amount on the credit meter. As the casinos hoped, most players now find that playing credits keeps their hands cleaner and is generally more convenient than inserting coins into a slot. The advantage to the casinos, of course, is that by speeding up slot play, the casino's take increases.

DID YOU KNOW...?

Instead of paying out coins, most modern slot machines keep track of winnings in the form of credits that can be converted to coins or a cash ticket by pressing the CASH OUT button. The accumulated credits can also be played..

TOKENS – THE PRESENT

In many Midwestern riverboat venues, such as in Illinois, Indiana, Iowa, and Missouri, the slot machines only accept casino tokens, not U.S. coins. This began in Iowa where the first gambling statute included a $200 per player loss limit. To enforce the law, a system was set up whereby each patron could purchase up to $200 in vouchers when entering a casino. The vouchers were then used to purchase gaming chips or slot machine tokens. The slot machines accepted only the casino tokens; if they accepted U.S. coins, gamblers could easily get around the law by carrying regular coins into the casino.

The loss limit law was ultimately repealed, but the tokens are still in use because the casinos like them. They know that most customers will not leave with a few leftover tokens in their pockets. Some will cash them in, but many will just drop them in a machine on their way out. Another reason the casinos like tokens is that they have fewer assets tied up in the coin hoppers of hundreds of machines. A quarter is worth twenty-five cents, but the tokens cost only pennies apiece to have minted. Consequently the token system improves the cash flow and other casino accounting numbers.

TOKENS – THE FUTURE?

To avoid the handling problems of six different coin denominations, some casinos are testing a new token system devised by some inventive Australians. Under this system, now commonly used in Australia, all machines, regardless of denomination, will accept only special dollar-value tokens. If you play a quarter machine, for example, the token will register as four credits. Now the coin counter in the change booth only has to handle the one denomination. Because of the popularity of cash tickets, tokens will probably not catch on in the United States.

CASH TICKETS

Another solution to the coin-handling problem is the use of cash tickets. When you cash out, instead of dumping a bunch of coins into the tray, the machine spits out a printed ticket. You may then bring the ticket to a cashier and convert it into real money, which is more convenient than toting around a bucket of nickels or quarters. For the casinos, the advantages are even greater. They no longer have to employ all the people who spent much of their time filling and emptying coin hoppers and spent the rest of their time keeping records on where the coins went. The lines at cashier cages move faster because buckets of coins don't have to be counted, and there aren't any jammed coin counters holding everybody up. Oh yes, the casinos do love the tickets.

Typical cash ticket used in many casinos.

The newest generation of cash ticket can be inserted into another slot machine as though it was real currency. These tickets have a printed bar code (see illustration) that the machine can read to register the appropriate number of credits. Although the tickets look as if they are easily reproducible with a copy machine, don't try it. Each one contains a unique numeric security code. Any attempt to use or cash a second ticket with the same code will set off alarms.

This completely coinless system is prevalent in tribal casinos, and most other casinos are installing it as well. When The Palms in Las Vegas opened its doors in 2001, all of its slot machines had cash ticket capability. Clearly, the use of cash tickets is rapidly spreading.

REEL GOOD ADVICE

Handle any cash tickets you receive as if they were actual cash. You should really handle them more carefully than that because they are printed on thin paper and are more fragile than greenbacks. Not only are they fragile, they usually expire in thirty days, so be sure to cash them in before leaving the casino..

Of course, this evolution toward cashless gambling will eventually lead to the use of smart cards that will credit and debit your account as you play. Such cards are currently under development and are expected to be similar to slot club cards. As you can well imagine, these coinless and cashless systems only benefit the casinos and are especially detrimental to compulsive gamblers.

CASHOUT AND HANDPAY

At some point in your slot play, you will want to cash out your credits. You must do this by pressing the CASH OUT button. Before pressing the button, however, note how much the machine owes you. Then, after it has finished dumping coins, check the credit meter again to be sure it registers zero. If it doesn't, then either the coin mechanism jammed or the hopper ran out of coins. This is the time to call an attendant by pressing the CHANGE or SERVICE button.

SLOT TALK

A handpay is a jackpot payoff or cashout that is made by an attendant rather than by the machine.

When cashing out, a machine will only dispense a certain maximum number of coins because of limitations in the coin hopper capacity. Depending on the denomination of the particular game, this number may be anywhere between five hundred and one thousand credits, as indicated by a sign on the cabinet. If the credit meter exceeds that number, pressing the CASH OUT button will bring an attendant instead of the expected clatter of coins. The attendant will first check the machine and then hand pay you with paper currency.

All jackpots of $1,200 or more must be hand paid by an attendant to meet the IRS requirement of submitting a W-2G form. Many smaller jackpots are also hand paid to keep from depleting the machine's coin hopper. For instance, on a nickel machine, a win of over $50 amounts to more than one thousand coins and will certainly be paid by hand. Whenever you receive a handpay jackpot, don't leave the machine without checking the credit meter for credits you may have previously accumulated. Then press the CASH OUT button to get what it owes you.

Finally, whenever you play the slots, be sure to carry some form of legitimate photo identification, such as a driver's license. For a payout of $1,200 or more, the IRS requires the casino to verify your identity for the W-2G form. If you do not have a photo ID in your possession (a slot club card will not do), you'll have to jump through a number of hoops to get your money.

GENERAL PLAYING ADVICE

The casinos make sure that playing a slot machine is a relatively simple procedure: you insert a coin or a bill, press a button or two to make the reels spin, and if the right symbols line up behind the payline, you win some money. If the winning symbols don't line up, you lose your investment and (the casino hopes) you try again. However, in the real world there is more to it than that, and this chapter covers those other aspects of slot play.

THE PLAYING ENVIRONMENT

When playing the various table games in a casino, the patrons soon learn that there are certain rules of etiquette and protocols that need to be learned if they are to avoid nasty stares from other players and admonitions from the dealers. To a certain extent, the same is true when playing slot machines. Although the slots are played individually, there are times when interactions do occur with other players. It may be self evident that the normal rules of etiquette and courtesy would apply, just as for any other endeavor, but some people need to be reminded what they are.

This may be because playing slot machines is different than ordinary activities, and the casino environment is different than ordinary environments. Just so that you know what is expected, I will explain the correct approach to use for some situations that may not arise in everyday life.

When you are looking for a suitable slot machine to play, do not crowd the other slot players. Slot machine play tends to be a solitary activity, so many patrons do not like a stranger looking over their shoulder while they are spinning the reels.

Before you sit down at a machine, be certain that it is not in use. Check that the person sitting one or two seats away is not playing more than one machine. Ask, if necessary. A cup on the handle, a purse or sweater on the chair, an inserted slot club card, or a burning cigarette are all signs that someone stepped away from the machine for a moment. Yes, it is foolish to leave personal belongs at a machine to reserve it, but that is what some people do.

If you want to reserve a machine while you go to the restroom, ask an attendant who will usually accommodate you by placing a RESERVED sign on the machine. If the casino is not crowded the attendant may even agree to reserve the machine while you go to dinner. However, the casino will not be happy if you reserve one machine and then go off to play another.

Although most casinos have an overabundance of security people, don't let that lull you into doing foolish things like placing your purse in the space between two machines. Always keep it on your shoulder or on your lap. Laying down rolls of quarters is also not a good idea; keep them in your pocket or purse. Always assume that there are opportunists hanging around in every casino waiting for you to let down your guard.

REEL GOOD ADVICE

Avoid bringing a purse when you go gambling. A fanny pack is more secure, but only if you keep it strapped securely to your body. As soon as you remove it, it is no safer than a purse. The best approach is to carry everything in your pockets..

Finally, successful players are aware that alcohol dulls a person's judgment. Consequently, most of them never drink alcoholic beverages during a playing session. They reserve this activity to celebrate a big win or bemoan their losses.

TIPPING

Let me say at the outset that I don't believe in tipping unless a service has been rendered in a particularly efficient and pleasant manner. In a casino, tipping is never required. You are in total control as to when, where, and how much to tip.

Something many people are unaware of is that if you give someone a large tip for an instance of extraordinary service, your tip will be shared with the other employees in that service group on that shift. To comply with IRS regulations, all tips must be pooled and taxes withheld by the employer before the remaining money is divided among the workers. So your big tip is first taxed and then the balance is split up evenly between all the workers in that group. Sometimes even the lowest level of supervision shares in the tip pool. This doesn't seem to bother some people, but it bothers me.

In a restaurant, the tipping situation is well defined. The 15-percent tip has become so standardized that many patrons leave 15 percent whether the service was good, bad, or mediocre. In a casino, however, there are large gray areas. So much so that many people overtip when tipping isn't even indicated.

Let's start with the change attendant. Change persons are not normally tipped for making change. So the conventional wisdom is that if a change person provides a special service, a tip would be appropriate. What sort of special service could she provide? I don't really know. Changing a hundred-dollar bill? But that's her job, and changing a hundred is not a particularly difficult task. This is probably becoming a moot point, now that almost all machines accept paper currency.

I've read in some books that you should tip a change person who directs you to a "hot" machine. Granted, that would be a special service, but how could she know which machines are hot? And if she really knows, why aren't her friends playing them? However, if you walked away from a game, inadvertently leaving your purse behind or some credits in the machine, and the change person chased you down, that would be worth a tip!

After winning a jackpot, you might tip the change person, just because you feel generous. But then, shouldn't you also tip the person who paid you off and the security guard who accompanied this person? How about the minimum-wage person who cleaned up the coin wrappers and the ashtrays around your machine? Should you tip all these people? Remember that you will probably pay taxes on your winnings. Any tips you give out will be pooled and taxed as well.

The other service provider that you encounter while playing slots is the cocktail waitress. This is a no-brainer. You normally tip her fifty cents to a dollar per drink, depending on her efficiency and the complexity of the drink you order. If you are playing a dollar machine, I suggest you tip at least a dollar or you will look like a cheapskate.

SLOT CLUBS

Most people believe there is no such thing as a free lunch. If you also believe that, then you haven't spent much time in the casinos of Las Vegas, Atlantic City or, for that matter, the rest of the country. Slot clubs actually give you more than a free lunch. You can get a free room, a free dinner, a free show, and you may even get some cash back. Of course, to get these comps you have to play the slot machines. But then, that's what you're doing anyway, so you might as well cash in.

How Did Slot Clubs Get Started?

The first slot club was opened in 1982 by the Sands Casino in Atlantic City. It was an attempt to establish better loyalty with the day-trippers, the large customer base that came from nearby urban centers and didn't stay overnight. The Sands adopted the concept of the airline frequent flyer programs, and the project turned out to be a resounding success. Soon after, the Golden Nugget (now called the Atlantic City Hilton) created a similar system using tickets and club cards. In 1984, Steve Wynn brought the Atlantic City Golden Nugget system to the

Golden Nugget in Las Vegas, and before long, other Las Vegas casinos were starting their own clubs and installing card readers on their slot machines.

Today, all casinos in Las Vegas and Atlantic City, as well as most of the rest of the country, are fully committed to their computerized slot clubs and consider them to be a major marketing tool. Player activity, which used to be very subjective, is now accurately tracked so that appropriate rewards can be given out in a fair and reasonable manner. These clubs depend entirely on computers, not only to track player activity, but to generate demographic data, identify gambling patterns, and quickly determine the popularity of new slot machines.

Some casinos have started using the term player's club instead of slot club because they use the same computer system to rate their table players. In those casinos, when you tire of the slots, you can sit down at a table game and continue adding to your point total. Just tell the floor supervisor what you are doing.

REEL GOOD ADVICE

Always join the slot club—there is no down side to doing this. Slot clubs operate on the same principle as frequent flier clubs. They are designed to encourage you to gamble in their casino by rewarding repeat players. A computerized tracking system keeps tabs on each player's activity so that comps can be awarded in a fair and consistent manner..

To Join or Not to Join

The question in some player's minds is whether or not joining a slot club is a good idea. Remember, the main purpose of the slot club is to buy customer loyalty, and any action that undermines that purpose would be self-defeating for the casino. With the possible exception of some tribal casinos, in almost every gambling jurisdiction, there is plenty of competition. Every casino needs your business and tries to keep you happy where you are so that you don't stroll down the block or go across the street. So long as a slot club is free of charge, you have nothing to lose, and there is no reason not to join. If you encounter one of the very few casinos that still charge for club membership, the best advice is to go somewhere else.

So, which casino slot clubs should you join? Join the club in every casino that you walk into intending to play the slots, and always join the club before you put a single coin or bill into a machine. Even if you end up not playing very long at a particular casino, it's worthwhile to join the club. First, it only takes a few minutes to do. Second, many casinos have a sign-up incentive, which you might as well take advantage of. Often this is a few free spins, free points, or a small gift. When a casino is running a special membership promotion, the incentive can be quite substantial, such as a loss-refund guarantee during a period of play, or a cash bonus. And finally, it puts your name on the casino mailing list so that you can be notified of special promotions and be offered incentives, such as a free room, to lure you back to that casino.

The most pervasive fallacy about slot clubs is that inserting a club card will reduce the payoffs on the machine. There are several reasons why this can't possibly be true. To begin with, the card reader is actually an add-on device that is completely independent of the machine's software. In fact, the slot machine computer doesn't know or care whether or not a card was inserted into the reader. Furthermore, the fallacy makes no sense because a slot club is designed to build customer loyalty, not destroy it. Even if a casino could change the payouts, why would it penalize its best customers?

As with many gambling misconceptions, there is also the reverse version that says inserting a club card will increase the jackpots. This is just as silly.

How to Join a Slot Club

How do you actually join the club? That's easy. When you enter the casino, head directly to the slot club desk or booth. If you don't see a sign, ask the first employee that you encounter for directions. When you get there, if there's a stack of application forms on the counter, take a few moments to fill one out before you see the clerk. The form will usually just ask for your name, address, and birth date. Some forms have a space for your social security number. Leave it blank—they don't need that information until you've hit a jackpot of $1,200 or more.

You'll also have to show them some form of photo identification (such as a driver's license) to verify your identity. The main purpose of the application is to record your mailing address so they can send discount coupons and information on special promotions. Some casinos don't use an application form—the clerk just enters the information into the computer directly from your driver's license. While you have the clerk's attention, ask how to earn points, what benefits are available, and how to redeem the comps. She will probably hand you a brochure. If she hasn't already told you, ask if there are special offers for new members.

Couples, married or not, should decide in advance whether or not to have a joint account. In a joint account, the point accumulation is combined for both persons, and can result in bigger comps. The advantage is mainly for couples who do not play much, and don't accumulate very many points. Normal players are usually better off with separate accounts. Even if they haven't accumulated many points, they may each get room and meal comps in the mail that they can combine for a longer future stay.

In some casinos, however, when a married couple comes to the slot club desk, the clerk will insist on creating a joint account, which can be difficult to change, later. The best way around this is for each spouse to sign up at a different time. On the application form, just be sure to leave the spousal information box blank.

After you are signed up, you will be issued a coded card so that the computer can track your playing habits. The more you play, the more points you rack up. These points can then be traded in for a variety of comps or cash rebates. Even if you don't use the card very much, the casino will notify you of slot tournaments and mail special offers to entice you to come back in and play some more.

What is a Comp?

The term comp is in such common usage that some of us forget that not everyone knows the exact meaning. It's simply a shortening of the word complimentary, which is something given in addition to what is expected. In a casino, it means something given free in return for your losses at the games so that you're more likely to return. It specifically refers to gifts given by the casino to good customers and usually refers to meals, rooms (or suites), show tickets, and even cash rebates. Big players may also be given clothing, outside entertainment, golf trips, spa treatments, and airfare.

When you accumulate a few points by using your slot club card, some of the comps are almost automatic. You may be given a brochure that lists what you can get, or there may be a comp store, where the merchandise is priced in comp points. However, there are some comps that you have to ask for. Say, the two of you have been playing the slots all day and you're starting to get hungry. No one is going to come over and offer you a free meal—you have to ask for it. Tell one of the slot attendants that you would like to speak to a casino host, and she will page one for you. Ask the host if you have enough points for a free meal. If not, ask how much more play would be required.

Whenever you ask for something, be sure to do it politely. If you get demanding, you'll find that you get fewer benefits because casino hosts have considerable discretion. The words *please* and *thank you* can go a long way in this situation.

When you are ready to check out, contact the host and ask if you qualify for a reduced room rate. Even if your room isn't free, you will at least get the casino rate, which is considerably lower than the rack rate. In many casinos, you will get the casino rate just for joining the slot club.

Giving away comps is one of the smartest marketing tools in the casino's bag of tricks. There are very few people who don't enjoy the recognition and the feeling of importance that comps give them. To avoid falling into the trap of playing longer than you intended just to get that feeling of importance, try to remember that the players getting the biggest comps are the ones who lost the most. In the long run, it would have cost them less to buy the rooms, the meals, and the show tickets outright, rather than with gambling losses. The casinos give out those comps to make you feel better about losing all that money, and to get you to return and lose more money in the future.

Inserting a Slot Club Card

Using the Slot Club Card

When you play a machine, be sure to always insert your card so that you can accumulate points. Every slot and video poker machine has a card reader that accepts slot-club cards. Remember, however, that the card has to be from the casino (or casino system) in which you are playing. When you insert the card, a screen display will greet you by name and may even tell you how many points you have accrued. When you leave the machine, remember to retrieve your card. If you forget or lose the card, however, don't be concerned—you can easily get another. In fact, most casinos will honor a request for two cards so that you can play two machines at the same time.

If you are a regular player, the comps from most slot clubs can add one half percent to the total amount of your wagers, and some will add as much as one percent. Some casinos offer a choice of comps or cash rebates. Many gamblers don't realize that these comps and rebates are not a function of your losses, but are based on the total action, which is much larger than the amount you actually risk. Casinos are not that concerned with short-term wins and losses, but operate on long-term percentages. Thus, they figure that the more you play, the more you will lose. How quickly the action (and your point total) can build up is revealed in the following example.

Let's say you start with $20 worth of quarters and spin the reels at the moderate rate of 400 times an hour. After just two hours of play at five coins a spin, you have cycled all 80 quarters through the machine 50 times. Whether or not you came out ahead, you generated $1,000 worth of action (800 spins at $1.25 a spin = $1,000). If there are two of you, that's $2,000, and if you played five hours, that's $5,000 worth of action, which will surely get you something in return.

Many people do not realize how little money has to be at risk to generate those comps and cash rebates. Be sure to take advantage of the available premiums by always using your slot club card.

10 IMPORTANT TIPS FOR SLOT PLAYERS

Tip #1. Be sure to always insert your slot club card.

In some casinos, using your card can effectively increase the payback of the machine you are playing by as much as one percent. You haven't joined the slot club? If you've read the section on slot clubs, you will know that there is no down side.

Tip #2. Play only what your bankroll can handle.

When you arrive at a gambling resort, you should first ascertain what denomination of machine you should be playing. To help you determine this, the following table shows how much bankroll is needed for a two-, three-, or five-coin bet in each denomination, assuming eight spins per minute and a 95 percent payout rate:

HOURLY COST OF PLAYING A SLOT MACHINE		
	2 COINS	3 COINS	5 COINS
Nickel machine	$2.40 per hour	$3.60 per hour	$6 per hour
Quarter machine	$12 per hour	$18 per hour	$30 per hour
Dollar machine	$48 per hour	$72 per hour	$120 per hour

Next, decide how many hours you expect to play over the course of your stay. For example, assume you start with a bankroll of $1,000 and would like to play an average of five hours a day for four days. That's a total of twenty playing hours. Dividing twenty hours into $1,000 gives a playing rate of $50 per hour. Thus, you should not play anything more costly than a two-coin dollar machine. In actuality, you may win more or lose more than the 95% payback would indicate, but at least you have a reasonable starting point.

Tip #3. When you insert coins, be sure to get what you pay for.

Like any equipment with mechanical components, slot machines are subject to considerable wear and tear. This is especially true of the coin mechanism. After handling hundreds of thousands of coins, the mechanism will malfunction sooner or later. Your best protection is to observe the glass and the paylines as you insert each coin to be sure the correct sections light up, showing that they are properly activated. If you hit a winning combination that doesn't pay because only two of your three coins registered, you are out of luck. If one of your coins doesn't register, be sure to wave down an attendant or press the CHANGE button and wait for someone to arrive. Don't spin the reels before the situation is rectified.

Tip #4. Play one machine at a time.

Slot managers know that some people like to play two slots simultaneously, so they usually flank a loose machine with tight ones on both sides. At best, you will win from a loose machine only to lose your winnings to a tight one; at worst, you will lose to two tight machines. Two loose machines are never knowingly placed alongside each other.

Tip #5. Never play the machine right next to someone who is winning.

If the winner's slot is loose, the machines on either side will be tight. Of course, the winner's machine may just be a moderate payer that turned hot, but you don't know that for certain.

Tip #6. Stay with a hot machine.

Never leave a machine that just paid a big jackpot. By definition, it is a hot machine that could continue to pay out very nicely. Don't abandon the machine unless it has not paid anything for six consecutive spins.

Tip #7. Observe other players who are winning.

Watch players who are winning regularly and keep an eye (and ear) out for sudden jackpot winners. For any number of reasons, these people may occasionally leave while their machines are still hot. If you see that happen (and your machine is cold), move over to the other machine before someone else gets there. Why would a person leave a hot machine? Many slot players think a machine turns cold after paying a big jackpot. Or maybe they have a dinner reservation or tickets for a show. If the machine is still in a hot cycle, their loss is your gain.

Tip #8. Abandon a cold machine.

Don't throw good money after bad. If, after six spins, the machine has paid out very little, abandon it. If available, move over to the slot right next to it. Tight and loose machines are often placed side by side.

Tip #9. Never leave a machine that owes you money.

Sometimes when you hit a big jackpot, an attendant has to make the payoff, or sometimes during a payoff, the machine's hopper runs out of coins. Occasionally a machine malfunctions and you can't redeem your credits, or the bill acceptor gets hung and eats your Franklin without giving you credits. Stay with the machine no matter how long it takes for an attendant or mechanic to arrive. If you leave the machine, you will have trouble claiming what is rightfully yours.

Tip #10. Don't forget to press the CASH OUT button.

Most machines accumulate credits as you play, and you must press the CASH OUT button to convert the credits into coins. Even if you have just won a hand-paid jackpot, before leaving the machine, press the CASH OUT button and be sure the credit meter reads zero. If it doesn't, call an attendant because the machine may need a hopper fill, or the coin mechanism may be jammed. If you are distracted when you leave your machine and forget to cash out, someone else will get to enjoy your winnings.

And finally, remember the cardinal rule of slot play:

QUIT WHEN YOU ARE AHEAD, BUT NEVER QUIT *WHILE* YOU ARE WINNING!

OPTIMIZING THE PAYBACK

With the exception of banking games (covered in a later chapter), playing slot machines is usually a losing proposition. All machines are intended to be profitable for the casino, and each one has a designed-in payback percentage. In many cases the payback is fairly good, but careless playing techniques can make it a lot worse. Knowledge of the machine payback helps players to avoid mistakes that result in a poorer than optimum return.

MICROPROCESSOR AND RNG

All slot machines today are microprocessor controlled. A microprocessor is the computer board inside the machine, which is the electronic brain of the game. It is very similar to the computer you may have at home, except that it serves the single purpose of controlling all the functions of the slot machine including the movement of the mechanical reels. In video slots, the screen is similar to the monitor on a home computer, except that it usually has touch-screen capability.

The random number generator (RNG) is one of the chips on the internal computer board. It generates thousands of random numbers a second, and each random number sequence defines a specific set of reel symbols. The instant a player presses the MAX BET or SPIN button, the next set of randomly generated numbers is selected.

DID YOU KNOW...?

In most gaming jurisdictions, new models and styles of slot machines have to be approved by the local gaming commission before they can be installed. The main concern of the gaming regulators is that the RNG in each machine is operating properly..

The program uses this set of numbers to define the symbol combination that will appear under the payline on the reels or on the video screen. A fraction of a second after the player hits the button, the program determines the final position of the reels—before the reels have even gotten up to full speed. Obviously, the actual spinning of the reels is window dressing since the outcome has already been predetermined.

By using this scheme, slot machines operate in a totally random fashion, and there isn't anything a player can do to change that. This is true for all currently approved machines in legal casinos in the United States, whether they have video screens or spinning reels.

MACHINE PAYBACK

The average amount of money that a slot machine returns to the player after a long period of play is called the payback. The payback is stated as a percentage of the amount that the player invested in the machine. If the payback is 95 percent, for example, you can expect to lose five percent of every dollar that you bet.

Thus, the casino is charging you an average of 5 percent (over the long run) for the privilege of playing its machine. That is, for every dollar you risk, the casino keeps a nickel. That doesn't sound too bad, but in many cases the charge can be 10 percent, or even 20 percent. The only thing that keeps this number from getting completely out of hand is the competition between casinos.

In the old days, by adjusting the number of symbols on the reels and by changing the payoff combinations, a slot machine could be made to pay back any desired percentage. Today, the payback is adjusted by changing a chip in the microprocessor, a procedure generally done at the slot machine factory. The payback usually ranges from 80 percent to 99 percent, except in New Jersey where by law slots have to pay back at least 83 percent. Keep in mind that these numbers are long-term averages. Machines that are set to the lower end of the range are considered to be tight, while those at the upper end are liberal or loose.

In most major gaming jurisdictions, the average paybacks actually range from around 90 to 98 percent. Historically, the highest-paying machines have always been in Nevada, where Reno/Tahoe and North Las Vegas are usually the best, with downtown Las Vegas not far behind. The average paybacks on the Las Vegas strip run neck in neck with most smaller jurisdictions such as those in Mississippi, Louisiana, and Illinois. Atlantic City, taking advantage of the largest population center in the United States, trails behind by one or two points.

The average paybacks also vary according to the machine denomination. The more you are willing to risk, the more the casino is willing to give back. When a player switches to a higher denomination, the casino makes more money and can afford to give more of it back. The following chart shows the approximate average paybacks in Nevada for the year 2010 (rounded to the nearest point):

AVERAGE NEVADA PAYBACKS IN 2010	
DENOMINATION	AVERAGE PAYBACK
Penny	90 percent
Nickel	92 percent
Quarter	94 percent
Dollar	95 percent
$5	96 percent
$25	97 percent
$100	98 percent

The penny and nickel games still have the poorest payback, but that is changing. Even on the penny progressives—yes, they have penny progressives—a wager of three hundred to five hundred pennies ($3 to $5) is usually required to qualify for the top jackpot. Consequently, many casinos don't treat these any differently than their other progressives.

Only a few years ago, the average for nickel payback was less than 90 percent. Penny and nickel machines have changed dramatically with the proliferation of forty-five- and ninety-credit video games. The average bet per spin on a forty-five-coin nickel game is over a dollar, which makes these games more profitable for the casino than the quarter machines. Consequently, some casinos have been raising the paybacks on nickel games higher than their quarter slots. And before long, it is expected that the average payback for nickel games will exceed the quarter, and maybe even the half-dollar machines.

Unlike video poker, however, there is no sure way to tell which slot machines are the best. The posted payout schedule on the machine is of little help without knowing how the microprocessor chip is programmed. Most players are not privy to this information. However, ways to offset this problem are covered below.

FINDING THE LOOSEST SLOTS

Unlike video poker machines, you can't look at the payout schedule on a slot machine and tell if it is loose or tight. And when a casino advertises that its slots pay back up to 97 percent or that some of its slots have a "certified" 98 percent payback, it's difficult to tell which of the hundreds of machines on the floor are the advertised ones. Actually, you can get in the neighborhood, but it's not nearly as precise as finding the best video poker machines. The secret is, as they say in the real estate business—location, location, location.

In every casino, the slot manager gives considerable thought to the placement of the slot machines. Therefore, to determine where the few loose slots are located on the casino floor, you have to think like the manager. An even better way is to get inside information directly from those slot managers—which is what I have done for you.

Years ago, it was generally known that the best slots were usually located in high-traffic areas—next to the main aisles or near the front entrance—where the greatest number of people would notice the flashing lights and ringing bells of a jackpot winner. Many old-time slot players remember that advice and still seek out machines in those locations. Times have changed, however.

Today, most slot managers place their loosest machines where the greatest number of slot players will see and hear them when they pay off. The idea is to motivate the serious slot players so they will keep feeding their machines in the hope that the next big jackpot will be theirs. Consequently, they locate the loose slots next to change booths, on elevated carousels, and anyplace in the center of the slot area where plenty of slot players will notice them when they pay off. Whenever loose slots are placed in a straight row of machines, they are usually one of the first three machines from either end, and never in the middle.

However, not all machines in these locations will be loose because there are always far fewer loose slots than tight ones. In fact, a typical ratio is 5 to 10 percent loose, 30 to 40 percent tight, with the remainder being midrange. The best you can do is find the general area where most of the loose machines are likely to be.

Sometimes the managers also put a few loose slots within sight of the patrons in cafes and coffee shops (but not where the entrance line forms) to encourage players not to dally over their coffee, but to get back to their machines. Keep in mind, however, that tight slots always flank a loose slot, even though the machines appear to be identical. This is done to thwart those people who like to play two side-by-side machines simultaneously.

REEL GOOD ADVICE

Avoid playing slot machines in places other than casinos. Machines located in stores, laundromats, restaurants, and airports are known to be poor payers.

It is almost as important to know where the tight machines are likely to be placed by the slot manager, so you can avoid them. Anywhere people stand in lines waiting to get into buffets or shows are prime locations for tight machines. Those people will kill time by idly dropping coins into the machines without really expecting to win—and they won't. Because many table-game players are distracted and annoyed by the constant clatter of coins, the areas surrounding the table games (especially baccarat and roulette) are populated with tight machines. The same is true of areas near the sports book. In fact, any location where the noise of slot machines would disturb nonslot players is apt to have predominately tight machines.

Finally, you must assume that all slot machines located outside of casinos, such as in convenience stores, grocery stores, laundromats, airports, bars, and restaurants, are very tight. In fact, they are probably the tightest machines in town.

PAYBACK CYCLES

During relatively short periods of play, the actual payback of a machine may be significantly higher or lower than the long-term average. Since you probably play a given machine for only a few hours at a time, your concern is for short-term rewards, while the casino is interested in long-term profits.

Consequently, from a short-term viewpoint, a slot machine is considered hot when it is paying out more than expected, and it is considered cold when it is paying less than expected. It is widely believed that most machines, regardless of how loose or tight they are to begin with, go through hot cycles and cold cycles. Thus, a hot, tight machine is better than a cold, loose one. The next section explains how to judge whether a machine is currently running hot or cold.

TESTING YOUR MACHINE

Once you have found a suitable nonprogressive machine, it is prudent to first run a simple test to judge whether it is hot or cold. Do this by playing through one roll of forty quarters ($10) allowing the winnings to collect in the tray or accumulate as credits. In a two-coin machine, this will amount to twenty spins. In a three-coin machine, you will get thirteen spins, with an odd coin left over. When the roll is finished, count the number of coins that have collected in the tray, or look at how many credits you have accumulated. If your winnings are at least 75 percent ($7.50) of what you invested, stick with the machine. If not, move to another machine and repeat the test. Of course, in a dollar machine, your investment will be four times as large, but the testing principle remains the same. In any case, if after the first six spins of the test you have won nothing, the machine is cold, and you should vacate it without carrying the test any further.

If your test winnings are at least 75 percent, but less than 90 percent, the machine is marginal and you may want to repeat the test to find out if it is in an up cycle or down cycle. Should the second test turn out better than the first, the machine is probably in an up cycle. This means the machine is getting hotter, and you should stick with it. Otherwise, abandon the machine. This test does not determine how loose or tight a machine is, but only if it is running hot or cold. Even tight machines have hot cycles.

REEL GOOD ADVICE

Keep in mind that a hot cycle has a limited life, even on a loose machine. Consequently, you should be prepared to quit a hot machine as soon as it appears to be turning cold. An important clue is that it hasn't paid off in six consecutive spins. In fact, the most conservative players will abandon their machine after five cold spins..

This testing procedure only applies to basic flat-pay machines, and not to progressives. The strategy with progressive slot machines is to go for the main jackpot, with little concern for smaller wins, as explained later.

KINDS OF SPINNING REEL MACHINES

On the surface, many reel spinners still look similar to slot machines installed in the early Las Vegas casinos over a half century ago. They have three spinning reels, and some of them still have a pull-handle on the right side, just like the old one-armed bandits. Inside the cabinet, however, they are totally different. They may have mechanical reels, but those reels are driven by electric stepper motors that are fully controlled by a microprocessor. The pull-handle, which used to engage gears and cams that mechanically spun the reels, now simply operates an electrical switch connected to the same circuit as the switch under the SPIN button. Many progressive machines are also reel spinners, but this chapter only covers games with a static (unchanging) top jackpot.

Although the variety of spinning reel machines may seem endless, they come in just four main styles. All other differences have to do with the kinds of symbols used and the amounts of the payouts. Following are the four basic types:

COIN MULTIPLIERS

In most casinos, multipliers are very popular machines. Multipliers are single-payline games where the number of coins bet on one spin multiplies the potential payouts. When this mathematical relationship is exact, the game is called a true multiplier. Bally's "Double Trouble" is an example of a two-coin true multiplier.

In most games, however, the top jackpot is higher than the multiple when the maximum number of coins is bet. This version is called a modified multiplier (see illustration). The purpose of a modified multiplier, of course, is to encourage the player to bet the maximum on every spin. For instance, on most three-coin multipliers, if the top jackpot pays one thousand coins for a one-coin bet, the second coin will pay two thousand coins, but the third coin may pay four thousand coins (instead of three thousand coins), or even five thousand coins or more. Hence, the conventional advice is to always bet the maximum number of coins. However, this is not necessarily good advice, as will be explained in the strategy section.

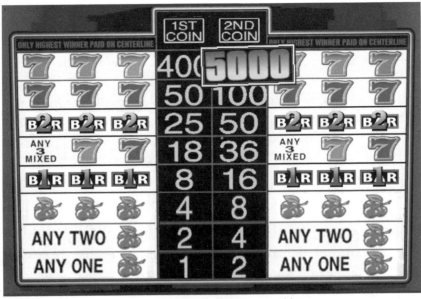

Typical modified multiplier paytable.

MULTI-LINE GAMES

As you stroll through the casinos, you will notice that there are plenty of reel spinners with multiple paylines. In the industry, they are called line games because the paytable is payline-driven. While a single-payline slot machine has one horizontal line across the window, a three-payline slot has two extra horizontal lines, one above and one below the center line. The extra paylines are activated by betting additional coins, giving you two additional chances of hitting a winning combination. Although you may activate one, two, or three of the paylines by inserting one, two, or three coins, to qualify for the maximum jackpot benefit, you must play all three coins.

Some machines have five paylines, with two of them crisscrossing the window diagonally, giving you a total of five winning chances (see illustration). These machines take up to five coins, one for each payline, and here again, you must play the maximum number of coins to qualify for the top jackpot. From the standpoint of return on investment, the multi-line slots are perfectly fine machines if you don't mind the higher bankroll requirement.

Slot window with five paylines.

REEL GOOD ADVICE

Don't assume that all machines with the same name are identical. The IGT game called Triple Diamond comes in several versions that have one, three, five, or nine paylines. Furthermore, the one-payline version comes as a two-coin or three-coin multiplier.

OPTION-BUY GAMES

Option-buy games are usually (but not always) single-payline games that may be called buy-a-pay, as well as various disparaging names. When you bet more than one coin, instead of multiplying the payout, these machines activate additional winning symbol combinations (see illustration). To get all the possible winning combinations, you must play the maximum number of coins. Unless you do so, the overall payback of the machine is seriously compromised. IGT's "Top Dollar" is an example of a typical option-buy machine. It comes in a two- or three-coin version, and you must wager the maximum to qualify for the top-box bonus of up to one thousand credits.

Some three-coin option-buy games can be misleading because the second coin is a multiplier, and only the third coin buys you additional symbol combinations. Therefore, on any game you are considering, study the paytable carefully because if is an option-buy, you must never bet less than the maximum.

Typical option-buy paytable.

So why would anyone call an option-buy game bad names? Because many people do not read the paytable carefully, and then they get annoyed when they bet one coin, hit a winning combination of symbols, and get paid absolutely nothing. If it was a multiplier, they would have been paid a reduced amount, but they would have won something. Most people tend to get upset when they finally hit a winner and then don't get paid. Don't let this happen to you. If you decide to play an option-buy game, be sure you always bet the maximum.

BANKING GAMES

Banking games are games in which points, credits, or some form of game assets are accumulated as they are played. They are designed to encourage players to continue playing until they eventually collect the banked bonus. Banking games may also have the paytable features of multipliers or line games.

Although some banking games, such as Piggy Bankin' and X-Factor, are reel spinners, more and more of them are video games with secondary bonus screens. The best strategy for profitably playing reel spinning banking games is basically the same as for the video versions. To keep all the detailed playing information for banking games together, the playing strategy for reel spinning versions is combined with the video versions in a later chapter.

VIDEO VERSIONS OF SPINNING REEL GAMES

The major slot machine manufacturers, such as IGT and Bally, supply some of their most popular machines in either a spinning reel or video format. These are three-reel slots and, except for the format, both versions are identical. They are multipliers, multi-line, or option-buy machines, so the information in this chapter applies to the video versions as well as the spinning reel versions. Slots that are marketed in both formats include Blazing 7s; Double Diamond; Red, White & Blue; Sizzling 7s; Triple Diamond; and White Lightning.

KINDS OF VIDEO SLOT MACHINES

The newest and glitziest slot machines on the casino floors display five or six simulated reels on a video screen. Although these games typically have nine to twenty paylines, there are some with up to sixty paylines that zigzag in almost every conceivable direction across the screen. On most machines, a bonus mode appears on a secondary screen when you hit the right symbol combinations. This bonus mode is the only real chance you have to recoup your losses and get ahead of the game. Other machines have a bonus banking mode to encourage you to keep playing in an attempt to reach the big bonus payout before your bankroll is totally depleted.

The most common games, however, have five reels, nine paylines, and encourage you to bet up to five coins per line. Because this adds up to forty-five coins, a maximum bet on a quarter machine costs $11.25 a spin—too rich for most players. Consequently, the nickel machines have taken on new popularity. At $2.25 per spin, the maximum bet on a nickel version is all most players are ready to contend with. Yet the casinos continue to display their greediness by putting more and more ten-coin-per-line nickel machines on the main floor. At $4.50 for a maximum bet, these nickel games are competing with the $5 machines in the high-limit area. As you play any of these computerized wonders, keep in mind that when you bet forty-five credits, and the machine loudly announces that you won thirty credits, *you are still losing money.*

Of course, none of this could happen if the nickel machines weren't more convenient to operate than they used to be. The days of buying rolls of nickels from the cashier and feeding them, one at a time, into the machine are gone. Now all you have to do is slip a bill into the currency acceptor and start to play. Of course, when you are ready to cash out, you still have to contend with that little coin bucket. Even this inconvenience is disappearing as machines spit out cash tickets instead of coins.

Because most video games have multiple paylines and accept multiple coins for each payline, they might be called multiplier line games. Within that designation there are two types of video games with distinctly different playing strategies: bonus games and banking games. A third category, called multi-game, is a machine configuration that is important enough to be treated separately.

BONUS GAMES

Except for the video versions of spinning reel machines, almost all video games have secondary bonus screens that pop up when you hit certain symbol combinations. The bonus screens often require some action on the part of the player, and always award extra credits. Examples are:

Choose Your Bonus

Three to five objects appropriate to the game theme appear on the screen. By touching the screen, you select one of them, which then displays the number of credits you have won. An example is Bally's "Boxcar Bonus."

Free Spins Bonus

A set of bonus reels with special symbols and multipliers appears on the screen. When the reels spin, a bonus is awarded for winning combinations, which may include additional bonus spins. An example is IGT's "Elephant King."

Match Play Bonus

A bonus grid with hidden symbols appears on the screen. By touching the screen, you select grid spaces to find matching symbols and multipliers, which determine the amount of your bonus. An example is IGT's "The Munsters."

Pick to Win Bonus

Items that hide bonus amounts are displayed on the screen. By touching the screen, you pick items that reveal bonus credits and multipliers. An example is WMS's "Monopoly."

BANKING GAMES

To the casual observer, banking games appear to be ordinary bonus games, in that a secondary screen is part of the mix. There is, however, an important distinction that puts them in a class by themselves. As the game is played, points or some form of game assets are visibly accumulated by the machine in a "bank." When the bank reaches a certain condition or the achievement of some goal occurs as a result of continued play, these assets are paid out in the form of bonus credits.

This feature is designed to entice players to remain at the machine longer than they intended in an attempt to reach the payoff goal. Regardless of this enticement, some players may quit the game before reaching the payoff goal. This leaves the game in a favorable state for any subsequent player who knows how to take advantage of it. Of course, you will learn how to do it in a later chapter.

MULTI-GAME MACHINES

This is a configuration where the player has a choice of several different games within a single game machine. Most multi-game machines, such as Bally's "Game Maker," include a mix of video slot games and video poker games. The video slot games may be of the bonus and/or banking variety.

KINDS OF PROGRESSIVE SLOTS

In progressive slot machines the top jackpot is not fixed. Progressives are usually part of a linked group of machines, and as the individual slots are played, the jackpot continually grows until someone wins it. After a win, the jackpot is reset to a base value and then begins to grow again. Some players are unaware that there is often a secondary jackpot, which is much smaller than the primary.

Progressive slots are typically two-, three-, or five-coin machines, although some video nickel machines will take as many as forty-five coins. In every case, the maximum number of coins must be bet to qualify for the top prize. Because progressives require a larger bankroll than basic flat pays, I don't recommend them for beginning slot players. The looseness or tightness of a progressive machine is entirely dependent on the current jackpot amount, since that determines the overall payback.

Progressive slot machines can be divided into three distinct categories. The categories roughly define how many machines are linked together (if any), and how large the progressive jackpots grow. As you will see later, the playing strategies for all the categories are quite similar.

STAND-ALONE PROGRESSIVES

At one time, all progressive slot machines were stand-alone. That was before someone thought of the idea of linking progressives together to make the jackpot meter tick up faster and higher. Most casinos still have stand-alones, the big difference being that the progressive jackpot is in the thousands of dollars instead of the hundreds of thousands or millions. Generally, you can identify a stand-alone by the lack of a large jackpot meter above the row or carousel. Instead, there is a meter on each individual machine, which doesn't change unless someone is playing the game.

LOCAL PROGRESSIVES

The first linked progressives were groups of machines within a single casino that were connected together so that they all contributed to a common jackpot pool. The size of a particular progressive group may be as small as a half dozen machines or as large as several dozen. Each cluster of machines has a large meter that displays the current value of the jackpot. You can tell it isn't a WAPS (see below) because the jackpot will be in the tens of thousands. If you are not sure, just ask an attendant or a floor supervisor.

WIDE AREA PROGRESSIVE SLOTS (WAPS)

Wide area progressive slots are the big money progressive machines. In 1986, IGT set up the first citywide linked progressive machines in Las Vegas and called them Megabucks. They were so successful that dozens of wide area progressive systems have been started since then— the majority being operated by IGT. On most of them, the top jackpot runs into the millions, which accounts for their enormous popularity. The idea of linking hundreds of similar machines within a single gaming jurisdiction—such as Nevada or New Jersey—has resulted in very high payouts and frequent winners.

CHAPTER 8 - KINDS OF PROGRESSIVE SLOTS

The individual casinos do not own the wide area machines. They are installed and maintained by a system operator such as IGT. When IGT sets up a new Megabucks machine, all the casino does is provide the floor space and take its cut of the action. IGT maintains the machine and all associated equipment including the interconnecting telephone lines. They handle all the needed administration and promotional activities, in addition to verifying and paying all the jackpots.

THE SIMPLEST SLOT STRATEGY

If you are a novice slot player and want to get started before reading and studying an entire book on the subject (such as this one), this short chapter will show you how to best do that. The only disadvantage is that you'll be restricted to playing only certain machines. Most of the slots that are striving for your attention will have to be ignored until you've learned more about the advanced strategy. Until you have done that, however, this simple strategy will work just fine.

CHOOSE A SIMPLE MACHINE

The best practice used by many experienced players when selecting a spinning reel slot is to stick to the basic three-reel nonprogressive machines. This is also the best advice for novice players. To stretch your bankroll, look for two-coin machines with a single payline. By sticking with a single-payline machine, you will know, without studying the paytable, that you are playing either a multiplier or an option-buy game (rather than a line game). By betting maximum coins or credits on a two-coin machine, you know that you will always qualify for the top awards. Therefore, for inexperienced players, this is the safest approach for a minimum investment.

REEL GOOD ADVICE

The novice slot player should look for a two-coin nonprogressive machine with three reels and a single payline. Betting the maximum on such a machine is the most economical way to assure that you will always qualify for the top jackpot..

If you find the paytables to be even the slightest bit confusing, heed the above advice. The more sophisticated techniques outlined in the advanced strategy chapters require you to fully understand the paytables for the various types of games. If you are looking for more variety, there is nothing wrong with playing the three- and five-coin machines, as long as you have a sufficient bankroll that allows you to always bet the maximum. Just remember that doing so will deplete your bankroll more quickly.

AVOID GAMES WITH HIGH JACKPOTS

Somehow avoiding games with high jackpots sounds contrary to what we are trying to do. Don't we want to win the biggest jackpots? Sure, but the chances of being successful are extremely remote. On some games with very high jackpots the chances of winning that jackpot can be worse than one in two million spins. Most of the time, it is much easier to win the top prize in a game with smaller jackpots. Furthermore, to keep the overall payback balanced, games with modest top awards will compensate by rewarding you with a greater number of small and medium payouts.

WHAT DENOMINATION?

The final decision you have to make is to select the correct denomination to fit your bankroll. This was covered in an earlier chapter, but for those of you who skipped to the simple strategy in this chapter, it is being repeated here.

CHAPTER 9 - THE SIMPLEST SLOT STRATEGY

First, decide how many hours you expect to play over the course of your stay. For example, assume you start with a bankroll of $1,000 and would like to play an average of five hours a day for four days. That's a total of twenty playing hours. Dividing twenty hours into $1,000 gives a playing rate of $50 per hour. Thus, according to the following chart, you should not play anything more costly than a two-coin dollar machine. In actuality, you may win more or lose more, but at least you have a reasonable starting point.

HOURLY COST OF PLAYING A SLOT MACHINE			
	2 COINS	3 COINS	5 COINS
Nickel machine	$2.40 per hour	$3.60 per hour	$6 per hour
Quarter machine	$12 per hour	$18 per hour	$30 per hour
Dollar machine	$48 per hour	$72 per hour	$120 per hour

The above chart shows how much of an hourly stake is needed for a two-, three-, or five-coin bet in each common denomination, assuming eight spins per minute and a 95 percent payback rate.

If you would eventually like to play a greater variety of games, including the video machines, you must read and study the following chapters on advanced strategy.

ADVANCED STRATEGY FOR SPINNING REELS

When most slot machine players take a vacation at a gambling resort, they allocate a certain amount of money for gambling. This allocated money is called their bankroll or stake. Some of the players lose their bankroll by the end of the first day, while others are able to stretch their bankroll to the end of their vacation. Some players even come home money ahead. It appears that some people are just lucky and others are not.

This may be true, but if the same people almost always lose and other people almost always win, there must be more than luck involved. The difference is that some people play haphazardly without thinking, while others play thoughtfully and methodically. Is there a thoughtful way to play a seemingly mindless game such as slots? You bet there is—and in the following sections you will find some shrewd and intelligent ways to improve your chances of coming out ahead.

STUDY THE GLASS

On a reel spinner, the paytable, known as the glass, is prominently posted above the reels. You should carefully examine this paytable before you actually start to play any machine. You may be surprised to note how different the payouts are from machine to machine, especially how much the top jackpot changes. Two side-by-side machines that appear to be basically identical (say, two-coin, one payline) may have top jackpots of 2,500 coins and 10,000 coins, respectively. Although it might seem better to play the one with the highest jackpot, to compensate for that jackpot, that machine will have fewer small and medium payouts. The overall paybacks of the two machines may, in fact, be very similar.

So which machine should you play? If you select the one with the large jackpot, you can't worry too much about small wins, because you are going for the big one. Just try not to be too disappointed when you don't hit it, because that top jackpot is at least as elusive as a royal flush in video poker. If you select a machine with a smaller top jackpot, your bankroll will last longer and fluctuate less because it will be regularly replenished with small and medium wins. Most players are more satisfied with such a machine.

Finally, before you start to play, check the glass to be sure you didn't inadvertently choose an option-buy game. This type of machine is not always obvious, especially those versions where the option-buy feature only applies to the last coin. If you really do want to play an option-buy game, be sure to read the section below on Multi-Line and Option-Buy Machines.

COIN MULTIPLIERS

As mentioned before, avoid games with high jackpots. The chances of being successful are extremely remote. For example, a very popular Bally game is Stars & Bars. One version of this game has a top jackpot of ten thousand coins, but the chances of winning it are one out of 262,144 spins. It doesn't take a math genius to figure out that at four hundred spins per hour, you would have to play over 655 hours to rack up 262,144 spins.

DID YOU KNOW....?

There is another version of Stars & Bars with a top jackpot of only 1200 coins, for which the chances of winning are much better: one out of 32,768 spins. In this case, the lower the top award, the better the chance of winning it..

After examining the specifications for different models of machines, this seems to be a general trend. Take a really high jackpot, such as the forty thousand coins found on French Quarters (fifty thousand in some versions). Here the chances of winning the top award are one in 2,097,152 spins! This is getting to be astronomical for a nonprogressive game. Of course, there is a mathematical reason why the program designers have to do this: to control the overall payback on the machine, these very high jackpots have to be made much tougher to hit.

REEL GOOD ADVICE

Play games with lower jackpots. To keep the overall payback balanced, many games with modest top awards will compensate by rewarding you with a greater number of small and medium payouts..

Therefore, the logical conclusion is that, most of the time, it is easier to win the top prize in a game with smaller jackpots, preferably no higher than three thousand coins. Playing these games has another advantage: most slot players go for machines with high jackpots, so the ones with low jackpots are more likely to be available in a crowded casino. In the next section, you are advised to look for true multipliers, and these games almost always have low to modest jackpots.

Bet one coin per spin. "But everyone says I should always bet the maximum coins to be sure I qualify for the main jackpots. In fact, you just said that in the previous chapter." Yes, I did. But that advice was for novice players and those who are not ready to read and digest this entire book.

I disagree with the advice to bet the maximum when it is given as a blanket rule. You will actually be money ahead by betting only one coin when you play certain machines, such as a true or near-true multiplier with a relatively low top jackpot (see illustration). This is the case even if you do eventually win that jackpot, which is a remote possibility.

Typical true multiplier paytable.

Betting a single coin on a three-coin machine cuts your monetary risk to one-third of what it would have been with a maximum bet. Such an approach may also allow you to move to a higher denomination, and higher denomination machines are generally a little looser. Thus, by applying some judgment in selecting your machine, you could get a better overall return by betting only a single coin or credit.

Although true multipliers may be scarce in some casinos, you shouldn't have much trouble finding a near-true multiplier. There are usually plenty of them around. These are machines where the maximum bet jackpot is only slightly greater than the coin multiple. The following chart gives some examples of what you should be looking for.

EXAMPLES OF TRUE AND NEAR-TRUE MULTIPLIERS					
	COINS	1st Coin	2nd Coin	3rd Coin	TYPE
IGT GAMES					
Double Diamond	3	800	1600	2500	Near True
Purple Passion	2	800	1600		True
Purple Passion	3	800	1600	2500	Near True
Spin Til You Win	2	500	1000		True
Triple Diamond	2	1000	2500		Near True
Triple Diamond	3	5000	10,000	15,000	True
BALLY GAMES					
California Dreamin'	2	800	1600		True
California Dreamin'	3	800	1600	2500	Near True
Diamond Winners	3	1000	2000	4000	Near True
Double Trouble	2	800	1600		True
Triple Gold	2	1000	2500		Near True
Wild Rose	2	800	1600		True

The 1st Coin, 2nd Coin, and 3rd Coin columns show the top jackpot for those games. Lesser payouts for all the listed games are exact multiples of the number of coins bet. Be careful when you check the paytables because some true and near-true multipliers also come in option-buy versions.

MULTI-LINE AND OPTION-BUY MACHINES

Avoid Games with High Jackpots

Avoiding high jackpots is the same advice I gave above for multipliers. It applies equally to multi-payline and option-buy games, and the justification is the same as for multipliers.

Always Bet the Maximum

Both multi-payline and option-buy machines penalize the player for not making a maximum bet, some more than others. Therefore, if you insist on playing these games, always bet the maximum, which in most cases will be two, three, or five credits. If you don't do this, you will be penalizing yourself.

ADVANCED STRATEGY FOR VIDEO BONUS GAMES

Because the new video games are significantly different than the old spinning reel machines, the best ways to play them are also different. Most video games use entertainment or personality themes to attract players. They may be based on television game shows such as Jeopardy or Wheel of Fortune, or they may be based on board games such as Monopoly or Bingo, or they may be pure inventions such as "Reel 'Em In" or "Filthy Rich." Whatever the case, try not to be influenced by the theme, but select a game on its potential first and entertainment value second.

Except for the exact spinning reel emulators mentioned earlier, most video slot machines have the bonus screen feature. To keep it as uncomplicated as possible, the following strategy for bonus games covers only the most common types of machines—those with nine paylines and a maximum bet of either five or ten credits per payline (see illustration). If you want to play a game with more paylines, try to apply the same basic principles described below.

Five-reel, nine-payline video screen

STUDY THE PAYTABLE

Unlike spinning reel machines, the paytables on most video games are not posted on the outside of the cabinet. You must press a button to bring the schedule up on the screen, which may be several pages in length. Consequently, most players never look at the paytable and play the game virtually blind. Unless you don't care about playing strategy, this is not a good way to go.

Before you start playing any unfamiliar video game, it is always a good idea to scrutinize the paytable. If nothing else, you should verify that the game is a true multiplier; that is, the payouts are multiplied by the number of credits bet and there is no special payoff benefit to playing the maximum number of lines and credits. This is the case for most of the games, but there are some that give a serious advantage for maximum bets. Avoid these because you lose all flexibility in your playing style.

There are two kinds of video multipliers, as shown below. One of them multiplies each win by the line credits wagered, and the other one multiplies each win by the total credits (line credits times the number of lines) wagered. Knowing the type of multiplier is necessary for determining the best way to play the game.

(1) **Line credits multiplier.** This type has a statement on the paytable such as: *All Wins are Multiplied by the Credits Bet per Line.*

(2) **Total credits multiplier.** This type has a statement on the paytable such as: *All Wins are Multiplied by the Total Credits Bet.*

A statement such as: *Scatter Wins are Multiplied by the Total Credits Bet*, does not necessarily mean the machine is a total credits multiplier. The statement, which applies only to scatter wins, appears in the paytable of most line credits multipliers as well as total credits multipliers. Since scatter wins are not line dependent, this has no effect on the playing method.

STRATEGY FOR LINE CREDITS MULTIPLIERS

When playing a line credits multiplier, the basic idea is to maximize the credits per line because that maximizes the amount of the payouts. For a given total wager, this is done by activating fewer paylines and betting more credits per line. The down side is that with fewer active paylines the hit frequency also drops off. The benefit is that unless you are playing a cold machine (and you should know better), an incremental betting sequence that varies the credits per line is simpler, and the bonus payouts are satisfyingly larger.

SLOT TALK

Hit frequency is the number of wins as a percentage of the total number of spins. A 20 percent hit frequency would be an average of one win for every five spins..

Start with Three Paylines

The payline choices on most nine-payline games are one, three, five, seven, or nine lines. Unless you are an old hand, resist the urge to hit the MAX BET button, which will commit you to a bet of ninety credits on some nickel machines. That amounts to $4.50 a spin! Even if your bankroll can handle higher denominations, until you get very familiar with these games, you should stick with the nickel machines.

To preserve your stake on a line credits multiplier, never start by betting all nine lines. If you start with only one line, however, the payouts are so infrequent that you may get discouraged before you win anything. No matter what the machine denomination, it is usually best to start with one credit and three lines. On a nickel machine, this only amounts to fifteen cents, or seventy-five cents on a quarter machine.

If you are losing after a dozen spins, try another machine. If, however, you have accumulated some credits, then start betting two credits. If you continue winning, increase your bet to three credits, and so forth. While doing this, you should activate only three paylines. You can play this way in an informal manner, or you can learn the betting sequence in the next section and use a more methodical approach.

Use an Incremental Betting Sequence

With so many choices of paylines and credits, you can make a total bet of as little as one credit or as high as forty-five credits. On a ten-credits-per-payline machine, you can make a one-credit bet or a ninety-credit bet. This leads to the idea of some form of systematic play to minimize risk and maximize gain.

One way of doing this is the sequence shown below, where the number of lines is kept at three while the number of credits is slowly increased. This progression for forty-five credits has many more steps than a common doubling system, and is easy to remember. The amount shown in the last column is the total cost per spin on a nickel machine.

SUGGESTED BETTING SEQUENCE FOR LINE CREDITS MULTIPLIERS			
NUMBER OF LINES	CREDITS PER LINE	CREDITS PER SPIN	TOTAL AMOUNT
3	1	3	$0.15
3	2	6	$0.30
3	3	9	$0.45
3	4	12	$0.60
3	5	15	$0.75
5	5	25	$1.25
7	5	35	$1.75
9	5	45	$2.25

There are two good reasons for increasing the number of credits per line faster than the number of lines. First, the chance of hitting a scatter pay is the same no matter how many paylines are activated. Second, when you get lucky and activate a bonus screen, the payout is multiplied by the number of credits per line. The number of lines has no effect on the total amount of the bonus.

Applying the Betting Sequence

The best way to apply the chart is to start at the lowest betting level (three lines, one credit per line). If, on your first spin, you win something (any amount) remain at the one-credit level and stay there until you win nothing. The first time you don't win (which may be the first spin), proceed to the next higher step by raising your bet to two credits per line.

At the two-credit level, you can take three possible actions:

(1) If you win nothing, remain at the two-credit level, and stay there until you have won nothing twice in a row. The rule is that you remain at any level until you have consecutively lost the same number of times as the number of credits per line.

(2) If you win an amount less than five times your total bet, remain at the two-credit level and restart the loss count in (1), above.

(3) If you win an amount greater than five times your total bet, drop back to the one-credit level at the top of the chart and start the sequence over.

Continue working down the chart in this manner until you reach the three-line, five-credit level. If at this point you are losing money, quit or change machines. Resist the urge to increase the number of lines until you are money ahead and then be sure to set a loss limit (see the Money Management chapter) to preserve the lion's share of your winnings.

There are now machines with fifty or more paylines. When you play one of those, be sure you progress to the maximum credits per line before you start to increase the number of paylines (unless the game is a total credits multiplier). Also, check the paytable to be sure that specific paylines do not have special payout bonuses.

STRATEGY FOR TOTAL CREDITS MULTIPLIERS

With a line credits multiplier, you activate fewer paylines and try to maximize the credits per line because that maximizes the amount of the payouts. The best playing method for total credits multipliers, however, is almost opposite from the method used for line credits multipliers.

Start with Maximum Paylines

With a total credits multiplier, you should always activate the maximum number of paylines and limit the total bet amount by cutting down on the credits per line. There is good reason for this. Instead of playing three lines at three credits per line, for a total of nine credits per spin, you should play nine lines at one credit per line, for the same total of nine credits. Although the total credits multiplier is the same either way (nine credits), with nine paylines activated, you will hit three times the number of wins. Since the total payout for each win is the same either way, you need to maximize the hit frequency by activating all the lines.

Use an Incremental Betting Sequence

Just as for a line credits multiplier, you should try to apply an incremental betting sequence. Since you should always activate all the paylines, the only betting variability is in the number of credits per line.

The simplest way is to start with one credit per line and incrementally increase it by one credit, say every three spins—you decide on the exact number. Thus, on a nickel machine, your first bet is forty-five cents (five cents times nine lines). Then increase the bet by one credit when you have three no-wins in a row. Anytime you hit a small win of less than five times your total wager, restart the three-count.

Another method is to incrementally increase the loss count as you increase the number of credits per line. You can make the loss count the same as the credits per line, or if you have a limited bankroll and are really conservative, make it double the credits per line.

The sequence shown below is for a nine payline, five credits per line machine. The number of lines is kept at nine, while the number of credits is increased incrementally. The amount shown in the last column is the total cost per spin on a nickel machine.

SUGGESTED BETTING SEQUENCE FOR TOTAL CREDITS MULTIPLIERS			
NUMBER OF LINES	CREDITS PER LINE	CREDITS PER SPIN	TOTAL AMOUNT
9	1	9	$0.45
9	2	18	$0.90
9	3	27	$1.35
9	4	36	$1.80
9	5	45	$2.25

Whenever you get a payout that is at least five times your total wager, restart the entire sequence at one credit per line. As an alternative, you may want to hold off by one spin before you restart the sequence, just in case you hit back-to-back wins. By restarting the sequence, you will help to preserve the amounts won. If you are fortunate enough to hit some nice bonus payouts, set a loss limit (see the Money Management chapter) and cash in when you reach it.

The above method is only one way of doing this. You should modify the sequence to fit games with more than nine paylines and/or more than five credits per line. You should also modify the overall procedure to fit your own personality because then you are more likely to stick with it. The only part you shouldn't change is the number of paylines. For games that are total credits multipliers, always activate the maximum number of paylines.

STRATEGY BENEFITS

Finally, I should clarify that the betting sequences suggested above do not convey any particular mathematical advantage to the player. Although they are not a magic formula for beating the system, they do carry the following benefits that will help to preserve your bankroll, reduce your losses, and help you come out ahead.

Applying a predetermined betting sequence forces you to play in a more methodical manner, rather than aimlessly hitting the buttons as fast as you can.

This methodical approach reduces your playing speed, which also helps to preserve your bankroll.

The sequence keeps your average betting level down, by starting low and gradually increasing your bet, thus reducing your overall investment risk.

The betting sequence helps to preserve larger wins by always making you return to the lowest betting level.

And most importantly, the methodical approach forces you to pay attention to the performance of the game so that you are more likely to stay with it when it is hot and abandon it when it goes cold.

MULTI-GAME MACHINES

Nearly all casinos have plenty of multi-game machines on the floor. The most popular are Bally's "Game Maker," IGT's "Game King," and Anchor's "Winning Touch." Each of these machines contains a variety of choices, which usually includes a mix of video poker, video bonus games, and video versions of reel spinners. Use the playing strategies described earlier for these games.

Some video banking games can also be found on multi-game machines. If the menu contains a banking game, by using the suggestions in the next chapter, you can determine ahead of time if it is worth playing.

Most of these machines are almost entirely touch-screen driven. Before committing any currency to one of them, you can surf your way through numerous screens to get instructions and paytable information on every game it contains.

BANKING GAME STRATEGY

Banking games are games in which points, credits, or some form of game assets are accumulated as they are played. They are designed to encourage players to continue playing until they eventually collect the banked bonus. Banking games may also have the paytable features of multipliers or line games.

Although some banking games, such as Piggy Bankin' and X-Factor, are reel spinners, more and more of them are video games with secondary bonus screens. The best strategy for profitably playing reel spinning banking games is basically the same as for the video versions, so they are treated here as a single category.

Many reel spinner banking games have a distinctive orange dotmation screen above the reels, but to the casual observer, video banking machines appear to be ordinary bonus games, in that a secondary screen is part of the mix. Banking games, however, have an important distinction that puts them in a class by themselves. As the game is played, points or some form of game assets are visibly accumulated by the machine in a "bank." When the bank reaches a certain condition or the achievement of some goal occurs as a result of continued play, these assets are finally paid out in the form of bonus credits.

This feature is designed to entice players to remain at the machine longer than they intended in an attempt to reach the payoff goal.

Regardless of this enticement, some players may quit the game (for any number of reasons) before reaching the payoff goal. This leaves the game in a favorable state for any subsequent player who knows how to take advantage of it.

WHY BANKING GAMES CAN BE BEAT

Unlike other bonus games, banking games have a unique characteristic that, if taken advantage of, can result in overcoming the normal payback percentage built into the machine. This can happen when a previous player has left a banking machine in a state of increased value, either due to ignorance, a lack of funds, a pressing engagement, or some other reason. Anyone who recognizes the potential value of the machine can then start to play it to advantage.

The advantage arises when some form of game assets have been saved or banked by the machine during a period of previous play. When the machine attains a certain condition or bonus goal as the result of resumed play, the accumulated assets are finally paid out in the form of credits. This will occur even if the resumed play is by a person other than the one who originally accumulated most of the banked assets. The trick is to recognize when an abandoned machine has reached the point at which continued play will likely be profitable.

SEARCH FOR BANKED CREDITS

Video slot machines that have a banking feature are not always apparent. To the casual observer, most of them just look like ordinary bonus games. The banking feature, however, is described on the paytable (which you can see by touching the paytable button on the screen), and the feature usually becomes apparent when you start playing the game. Therefore, you can eventually find a banking game by walking from machine to machine and bringing up and reading the paytable on each one.

Reel spinning banking machines are a little more obvious. They often have a top box with some type of dotmation graphic display.

In any case, I'll save you some time and trouble by listing a number of the most common video and reel spinning banking games in the next section, along with suggestions as to when they have attained a profitable state.

Since the banking feature has been around for a few years, many experienced slot players know the potential value of banking games and have learned how to take advantage of them. Sadly, a few unscrupulous types have used techniques for encouraging a player to leave a machine when it reaches a valuable state. Casinos are aware of this and do not look kindly on such activities.

Keep in mind that it is not good form to look over the shoulder of someone who is playing a banking slot, hoping that he will abandon the game. Casinos generally don't care who plays their slot machines or who wins the bonuses, but they have been known to bar individuals who harass or annoy other slot players. Before you sit down at a machine, take a moment to ensure that the machine has really been abandoned.

REEL GOOD ADVICE

Before you start to play, study the paytable and playing directions very carefully because some banking games get rather complicated in the way the bonuses are banked. You need to know that you are playing correctly, or you may lose the advantage that you started with.

MACHINES TO LOOK FOR

Useful information for playing some of the most popular banking games is provided below. The playing advice is as current as I could make it, but be aware that manufacturers frequently modify their machines and you should try to verify that the game you are considering is the same one as described. Applying the following suggestions does not guarantee that you will be money ahead every time you play an advantageous machine, but only that your long-term average will be profitable.

BINGO

This is exactly like the game using cardboard bingo. The video screen displays five reels that represent the five columns on a standard bingo card. Most of the time, the machine plays like any five-reel video game, but every so often a bingo ball appears on one of the columns and the machine will draw a bingo number. This continues until the selected bingo configuration is completed, whereupon a bonus round determines how many credits have been won.

Study the paytable on the machine to learn how to identify the various bingo configurations.

Strategy

Bet one credit per spin on one payline if you find a game in which the bingo is at least half finished. Although Bingo has five paylines, the bingo ball does not have to fall on a line to be valid. Cash out when the banked bonus is won.

BOOM

This game banks firecrackers and awards the bonus when 50 are accumulated. Although it is a five credits-per-payline, nine-payline game, don't ever bet 45 credits.

Strategy

Bet one credit on one payline when you find a game with at least 30 firecrackers lined up across the top of the screen. Cash out when the banked bonus is won.

CHUCK WAGONS

In this game of racing chuck wagons, if Your Wagon reaches the bonus area before Their Wagon finishes, you collect the banked bonus. The race distance is 70 miles.

Strategy

Bet maximum credits per spin when you find a game in which Your Wagon has gone at least 30 miles and Their Wagon is at least 25% behind Your Wagon. Cash out when the banked bonus is won.

DIAMOND THIEF

This is a rather complex three-reel game with the ultimate goal of filling all nine compartments of a case with diamonds, six diamonds per compartment, for a total of 54 diamonds.

Strategy

Bet one credit per spin when you find a game that needs no more than five diamonds to completely fill the case. Cash out when the banked bonus is won.

DOUBLE DIAMOND MINE, TRIPLE DIAMOND MINE

In these games, a bonus is paid when ten diamonds are accumulated in any of the three mineshafts.

Strategy

Bet one credit per spin when you find a game with nine diamonds in one shaft, eight diamonds in two of the three shafts, or at least seven diamonds in each of all three shafts. Cash out when the game no longer meets any of the above three conditions.

EMPIRE, EMPIRE KING

In these games, King Kong has to climb the Empire State Building a certain number of stories within a certain time limit. In Empire, the first bonus level is 70 stories; in Empire King, the bonus level is 90 stories. Study the paytable to get the details.

Strategy

Bet the maximum credits per spin when you find a game with at least twice as many seconds left on the timer as there are stories remaining for King to climb. Cash out when the distance counter resets to zero.

FISHIN' FOR CASH

This is a fishing version of Double Diamond Mine. Whenever a fish appears on the payline, it is reeled in and piled on one of three stacks.

Strategy

Bet one credit per spin when you find a game with nine fish in one stack, eight fish in two of the three stacks, or at least seven fish in each of all three stacks. Cash out when the game no longer meets any of the above three conditions.

GREASED LIGHTNING

This is a version of Chuck Wagons, where '57 Chevys are raced instead of chuck wagons.

Strategy

Bet maximum credits per spin when you find a game in which Your Car has gone at least 30 miles and Their Car is at least 25% behind Your Car. Cash out when the banked bonus is won.

ISLE OF PEARLS

This is a variation of Empire where you go down instead of up. To get the bonus, a pearl diver needs to descend at least 70 feet before time runs out (100 seconds).

Strategy

Bet the maximum credits per spin when you find a game where the diver has gone at least 30 feet and there are at least twice as many seconds left on the timer as there are feet remaining for the diver to descend. Cash out when it is obvious that the diver will not reach 70 feet before the time runs out.

JUNGLE KING

This is the opposite of Isle of Pearls, where the Jungle Man needs to climb up a vine a distance of 70 feet within 100 seconds.

Strategy

Bet the maximum credits per spin when you find a game where there are at least twice as many seconds left on the timer as there are feet remaining for Jungle Man to climb. Cash out when the distance counter resets to zero.

MERLIN

This is another clone of Empire with Merlin trying to reach a castle before time runs out.

Strategy

Bet the maximum credits per spin when you find a game with at least twice as many seconds left on the timer as there are units remaining for Merlin to travel. Cash out when the distance counter resets to zero.

PIGGY BANKIN'

Piggy Bankin' was the original banking game, and it caused quite a stir among the experts and analysts when this three-reel machine was first introduced. It also established WMS Gaming as a major competitor in the slot machine business.

Strategy

In Piggy Bankin', whenever you get three blank spaces on the payline, your bet is added to the contents of a piggy bank. Then, when the Break the Bank symbol lands on the right-hand payline, the contents of the piggy bank are yours. Bet one credit per spin when you find a $1, $2, or $5 game with at least 25 credits, or a nickel or quarter game with at least 30 credits in the bank. Cash out when you break the bank.

BIG BANG PIGGY BANKIN'

Big Bang Piggy Bankin' is a newer version of the Piggy Bankin' game (above).

Strategy

In Big Bang Piggy Bankin', you have to get three Break the Bank symbols (or wild equivalents) to win the banked bonus. Bet one credit per spin when you find a game with at least 50 credits in the bank. Cash out when you break the bank.

RED BALL

This three-payline nickel machine displays two 3 by 3 matrix squares alongside the video reels. The idea is to fill one of the squares with red balls and the other with black balls. Under each square is a number indicating the amount of the payoff bonus for completing that square.

Strategy

Bet one credit per line per spin (a total of three credits) when you find a game with at least a 20 under either square or at least a 15 under both. Cash out when the game no longer meets the above conditions.

SHOPPING SPREE

This game banks frequent shopper points, and the banked bonus is paid when 50 points are accumulated.

Strategy

Bet two credits per spin when you find a game with at least 30 frequent shopper points already registered. Cash out when you win the bonus.

SUPER 7S

This five-payline game is found on Game King machines, and the banked items are square sevens, that is, each seven is inside of a square.

Strategy

Bet one credit per line per spin (a total of five credits) when you find a game with at least three square sevens showing. Cash out when you win the bonus.

TEMPERATURE'S RISING

The idea is to raise the temperature on a large red thermometer to the bonus level. The heat goal depends on the particular machine version, but is plainly shown.

Strategy

Bet one credit per spin when you find a game where the amount of the bonus is greater than the number of degrees needed to "break" the thermometer. Cash out when the bonus is won.

TRIPLE CASH WINFALL

This is a money version of Double Diamond Mine, where coins fall on one of three stacks.

Strategy

Bet one credit per spin when you find a game with nine coins in one stack, eight coins in two of the three stacks, or at least seven coins in each of all three stacks. Cash out when the game no longer meets any of the above three conditions.

TRIPLE DIAMOND BASEBALL DIAMOND

Ballplayers move around the bases as you hit a single, double, triple, or home run on the third reel of this machine. The runs are accumulated and are paid out when you get a home run.

Strategy

Bet one credit per spin when you find a game with at least 25 accumulated runs plus the runs shown over the baserunner's heads. Cash out when the baserunners are cleared by a home run.

WILD CHERRY PIE, WILD CHERRY BONUS PIE

Through a rather convoluted process, a total of 54 cherries have to be accumulated in a nine-section pie.

Strategy

For Wild Cherry Pie, bet one credit per spin when you find a game with at least 44 cherries in the large pie. For Wild Cherry Bonus Pie, bet one credit per spin when you find a game with at least 48 cherries in the large pie. Cash out when the pie is filled and the bonus is paid.

X-FACTOR

The X factor is a payout multiplier that starts at 2X and can build as high as 10X. Whenever you choose to use the multiplier, it resets to 2X.

Strategy

Bet the maximum credits per spin when you find a game with an X factor of at least 6X. Cash out when the multiplying factor has been used.

PROGRESSIVE STRATEGY

The vast majority of progressive players are primarily interested in winning the top jackpot. These players consider the smaller wins to be useful only for replenishing their bankrolls so they can stay at their machines for a longer period of time. To support the large progressive jackpots, the machines are programmed so that the medium and small wins occur less often than in non-progressive games. If you have this all-or-nothing mentality, then the progressives are your game.

STAND-ALONE AND LOCAL PROGRESSIVES

If you like the idea of big jackpots but would prefer something less elusive than what the wide area progressives offer, you might be interested in trying a local bank of progressives. If the amount on the progressive meter is less than $100,000, then it is most likely part of a local group. If you are not sure if a particular row or carousel is local or WAPS, ask a floor supervisor.

REEL GOOD ADVICE

Play a stand-alone or local progressive slot machine if you prefer that the main jackpot always be paid in a lump sum..

Look for High Jackpots

The only strategy is to find a linked group of machines that is displaying a high amount on the progressive meter. This is not difficult because the present value of the top jackpot is prominently displayed on a large digital sign above each bank of machines, the number continually ticking upward as the players insert coins. If there is a secondary jackpot, it is shown on a smaller meter below the top jackpot sign.

Each time the jackpot is won, the amount on the meter is reset to a base value. Whenever a progressive meter is close to the base amount, it means there was a recent win and the next win is not likely to occur for some time. You should always try to find a group of machines where the meter shows the greatest dollar increment over the reset value. To find out what that reset value is, you will have to ask a supervisor. Just remember that when you play any kind of progressive, you must always bet the maximum if you expect to qualify for the big jackpot.

There are individual stand-alone machines with progressive jackpots that are often no higher than many of the non-progressive slots. There doesn't seem to be any valid reason to play these machines. If you do, be sure to find one in which the jackpot has been run up by other players, and bet the maximum.

Bet the Maximum Coins or Credits

No matter what else you might do, when playing a progressive always bet the maximum. It is the only chance you have of beating the system. If you don't bet the maximum coins or credits, you cannot win the progressive jackpot—and if you don't have a crack at the top jackpot, the overall payback on the machine will be rather poor. If you don't want to risk that much money, you are playing the wrong machine and you should find one of a lower denomination. Or you shouldn't be playing progressives at all.

WIDE AREA PROGRESSIVE SLOTS (WAPS)

The jackpots on WAPS, which can be a lifestyle-changing amount of money, are seldom won—so seldom that when someone gets lucky, it is always reported in the newspaper. WAPS have to be approached with a totally different attitude. That is, you can't mind blowing your entire bankroll on the infinitesimal chance of hitting a gigantic payday. It's something like playing the state lottery on a continuous basis. And you know what they say about most state lotteries; your chances of winning the big one are statistically the same whether or not you buy a ticket.

Furthermore, besides feeding a percentage of the receipts to the progressive jackpot escrow account, both the WAPS operator (such as IGT or Bally) and the casino in which the machine is located, take their cut. Consequently, the overall payback to the player is always less than 90 percent, often much less. For this reason, I don't recommend playing them. The odds of winning the progressive jackpot itself are so poor that every time you hit the SPIN or MAX BET button, you are literally throwing your money down a black hole. How can this be any fun?

For those of you who still insist on playing these machines, be sure you always bet the maximum coins or credits, or you will have a zero chance of winning the top jackpot. Although some WAPS have been known to hit just above the reset amount, I still recommend that you wait until the progressive meter gets at least twice as high. Though I hate to encourage you, I have provided some basic information on the most popular progressives that can be found in most jurisdictions.

Megabucks

The mother of all WAPS, these dollar slots have been around since IGT installed the first ones in 1986. The first Megabucks progressive jackpot was hit on February 1st, 1987 in Reno, Nevada for nearly five million dollars. These machines may be found in most casinos within each major gambling jurisdiction such as Nevada and Mississippi, as well as in tribal casinos. All the machines in a given jurisdiction are linked to the same huge jackpot pool.

Megabucks is usually a three-coin, four-reel machine, so you have to invest $3 on each spin to qualify for the primary jackpot. Line up the four Megabucks symbols on the payline and you win a multimillion dollar jackpot that is paid out in annual installments. After a win, the primary jackpot is reset to $7 million (in Nevada), and the secondary jackpot is reset to $2,000.

In 1990, IGT set up a Megabucks WAPS network in Atlantic City. It never was very profitable for the operators, which some analysts blamed on the nature of the Eastern gaming market. For many years, in an attempt to improve revenues, IGT did some serious adjusting and fiddling. They changed the number of reels and raised the reset amount, but they could never find the formula for success. In 2002, they finally gave up and shut down the system. In Nevada, however, Megabucks has never been more popular.

Wheel of Fortune

Another IGT success story, this three-reeler is now the most popular of all WAPS. It comes in four denominations, and requires the maximum number of coins to win the progressive, as follows:

COINS NEEDED TO WIN PROGRESSIVE	
Quarters	Three coin max bet and $200,000 reset
Halves	Three coin max bet and $500,000 reset
Dollars	Three coin max bet and $1 million reset
Five dollars	Two coin max bet and $1 million reset

The top payouts are made in annual installments for all denominations, which is common for IGT WAPS machines.

Wheel of Fortune Video

The video version has five simulated reels and is found in most jurisdictions except Nevada. It comes in penny, nickel, and quarter denominations.

Betty Boop's Big Hit

This is Bally's most popular WAPS, and it has some unusual features. First, most of the machines are multi-denominational; you feed a bill into the currency acceptor and then decide if you want to play nickels, quarters, or dollars. Second, in one carousel there are usually several theme variations, such as Swing Time Betty, Betty Boop's Double Jackpot, and Betty Boop's Roaring 20s.

To qualify for the progressive jackpot, you have to bet five nickels, three quarters, or two dollars. If you think you can beat the system by betting just five nickels, think again. According to Bally, the machines are programmed so that a player who bets two dollars has an eight times better chance of hitting the top jackpot than the player who risks only twenty-five cents by betting five nickels. Furthermore, the overall theoretical payback rises as the denomination goes up: 84, 86, and 88 percent for nickels, quarters, and dollars, respectively. After someone hits the progressive, the machine is reset to $100,000, and the winner is immediately paid the entire jackpot (less taxes).

Quartermania

As the name implies, this IGT WAPS accepts quarters, although it takes two of them to qualify for the big payoff, which is paid in twenty annual installments. The primary reset is $1 million, while the secondary is restarted at a measly $1,000.

Jeopardy

Jeopardy is basically a quarter machine except in Atlantic City where there are also fifty-cent and dollar versions. This is another IGT machine, so it pays the top jackpot in annual installments.

Jeopardy Video

Jeopardy also comes in a video version. It is a nickel machine with a reset of $100,000. Because you have to bet forty-five credits to qualify for the progressive payout, it is more expensive to play than the non-video three-reel version.

Elvis

This is another popular three-reel IGT game, which sports a bonus feature that plays Elvis tunes. It comes in two denominations with the following specifications:

ELVIS GAME SPECIFICATIONS	
Quarters	Three coin max bet and $100,000 reset
Dollars	Two coin max bet and $250,000 reset

The jackpot is paid immediately on both the quarter and dollar versions.

Millionaire Sevens

This popular Bally WAPS started in Nevada, but has spread to other jurisdictions. These are dollar machines with a reset of $1 million.

ODDS AND ENDS

Just when I think the entire subject of slot machines has been covered, there are still a few odds and ends left over that don't seem to fit in any of the previous chapters. Yet, the topics of misconceptions and slot tournaments are important enough that they should be included.

SLOT MACHINE MISCONCEPTIONS

During the hundred-odd years that slot machines have existed, many myths and fallacies have built up around them. If you have been reading this book with reasonable care, you will not be misled by the many stories and rumors that circulate among avid slot players. Nevertheless, to keep you from straying down that delusional path of old wives' tales, I will try to debunk the most persistent of the slot legends.

1. When jackpot symbols start appearing just above or below the payline, the machine is ready to hit a big one.

False. Slot machines were originally designed so that you could only see the symbols that fell right on the payline. The fact that you can see above and below the payline is a deliberate design feature. It invites you to wonder what might have been and is called wishful thinking.

This is part of the overall psychology used by casinos to encourage you to keep playing.

2. You are more likely to win if you pull the handle instead of pressing the MAX BET or SPIN buttons.

False. In modern slot machines, when there is a handle, it is connected to an electrical switch that activates the same circuit as the switches under the MAX BET and SPIN buttons. In other words, the electrical circuits in the machine don't know whether you pulled the handle or pushed a button. Pull handles are fast disappearing, so this will soon become a moot point.

3. The loosest slot machines are located near the entrance and on the main aisles.

False. This is a long-held belief among slot players, so those machines are usually pretty busy. The slot managers also know this myth, so many of them put tighter machines in those locations, knowing they will get played anyway. To learn where the loosest machines are located, read the section on finding the loosest slots.

4. If someone hits a jackpot at a machine you just left, that would have been your jackpot if you had stayed with it.

False. All modern slot machines contain a random number generator (RNG) that controls the outcome of each spin. While the machine is idle, the RNG spawns thousands of numbers every second until someone hits the SPIN or MAX BET button. Consequently, if the person who sat down at the game you just left hesitated a split second before spinning the reels, she probably would not have won that jackpot.

5. After a machine pays a big jackpot, it will run tighter for a while to make up for the loss.

False. The RNG does not have a memory. It just keeps on spitting out random numbers as though nothing had happened. In fact, it is theoretically and statistically possible for a machine to hit a big jackpot twice in a row.

6. Casinos can flip a switch to reset the slot machines to pay better or worse on weekends or nights.

False. There is no switch. To modify the payback of a machine (making it looser or tighter) would require changing a chip in the machine's microprocessor. To legally do this requires prior approval from the gaming commission, and the actual modification usually has to be performed by a factory mechanic while being observed by an agent of the gaming commission.

7. When someone hits a jackpot, a slot mechanic often opens the machine and resets the payback percentage to a lower value.

False. Modifying the payback is not a simple procedure. See above.

8. If an attendant or mechanic opens your machine for any reason, it will stop paying off.

False. The slot mechanic is your friend; his job is to make sure the machine is operating properly. He cannot affect the payoffs in any way. Neither can the attendant who clears a coin jam or refills the coin hopper.

9. A slot machine will pay off less (or more) if you insert the casino's slot club card.

False. The slot club card reader has no effect on the operation of the machine. Don't deprive yourself of this major benefit that can get you valuable comps and even cash rebates.

10. If you use a slot club card, the casino will report your winnings to the IRS.

False. The legal requirement is that the casino must report single wins of $1200 or greater, and they will do this whether or not you have been using a slot club card. The casino does not add up smaller wins and report them—why should they if they don't legally have to?

11. A machine will pay better (or worse) if you insert paper currency rather than coins.

False. The RNG determines the outcome of the next spin, and it does not know whether you inserted a bill, dropped in a coin, or played a credit. Nor should it care. Nor should the casino care.

12. A slot machine will pay better if you use cold (or hot) coins.

False. This is a very old myth, and it is so silly that it doesn't deserve a response. However, it keeps recurring and doesn't seem to want to die. Just be aware that there are no temperature sensors in the coin mechanism (why should there be?), so the machine doesn't know if the coins you are inserting are hot or cold. In fact, the RNG doesn't even know whether you inserted a coin, a bill, or played a credit (see above).

SLOT TOURNAMENTS

We know that there are poker tournaments and that there are blackjack tournaments, and we also know that the most skillful players usually win. But what in the world is a slot tournament? What skill do slot machine players apply to win such a tournament? The fact is, the only skill needed in a slot tournament is the ability to hit the SPIN button as rapidly as possible. The more reel spins that can be achieved in the allotted time period, the more winning points or credits are likely to be achieved.

Actually, most slot tournaments are nothing more than casino promotions. As such, they are usually a good deal for the contestants, especially the 100 percent equity tournaments, where all the entry fee funds are returned to the contestants in the form of prizes. Although the rules vary from casino to casino, prizes are often awarded to the top ten winners, along with a booby prize. Additionally, casinos often give the players free buffets, T-shirts, and other goodies.

If you are interested in tournament play, be sure to join the slot clubs of your favorite casinos. They will then notify you of future tournaments and how to sign up. When you are trying to decide where to play, look for a cashless tournament with 100 percent equity. Cashless means that your only monetary risk is the entry fee—the actual slot play costs you nothing.

Of course, when casinos do anything that seems to be a bargain, they eventually expect a payoff. By bringing all these slot players together, they hope that the contestants will be practicing on the other slots in the casino when they are not playing in the tournament. In fact, it can be so lucrative for a casino, that some of them even offer free tournaments to their active slot club members. This is just another good reason to join the slot clubs.

VIDEO POKER BASICS

Although video poker was introduced in the 1970s, these games didn't get popular until the 1980s. By the 1990s, many slot players realized that video poker had become the most liberal type of slot game on the casino floors. Consequently, its popularity surged until it became a major segment of the slot machine business.

Video poker is a machine version of a popular form of poker called five-card draw or, more simply, draw poker. In the most common version of video poker, a five-card hand is randomly dealt by the machine. The player then gets to discard any or all of the cards in the dealt hand, which are replaced by new ones. Choosing which cards to hold and which to discard to maximize the payback requires correct playing strategy. There are a number of game variations, but almost all of them are based on a one-time replacement of any of the cards in a five-card hand.

It is easy to find standard video poker machines that pay back more than 98 percent and some that pay back more than 100 percent when perfect playing strategy is applied. Whereas the payback of any particular traditional slot machine is a mystery, this is not true of video poker. Every video poker machine has its complete payout schedule posted on the video screen or on the glass display above the screen. Using this information, the overall payback of that machine can be computed.

To take full advantage of the potentially high payback in video poker requires two important actions. The first is finding a video poker machine with a payout schedule that provides a high payback. The second is using the best strategy when playing that machine. It is the purpose of this chapter to provide the information needed for a player to do both in a simple and effective manner.

VIDEO POKER VS. DRAW POKER

Video poker is fundamentally a one-player video representation of draw poker. Aside from the fact that all the action occurs on a video screen, video poker has some significant differences from draw poker. To avoid falling into serious traps while playing video poker, it is important to be aware of these differences. This is especially true for players already familiar with draw poker, since they have likely developed particular playing styles and habits. Although the two games have many similarities, the playing strategies are quite different.

The most important point in video poker is that you are playing against a machine with a fixed payout schedule, and there are no other players at the table. In table poker, if your hand is better than that of every other player at the table, you win the entire pot. You could win with a very poor hand, if that is the best there is—or you could lose with a very good hand if someone else has a better one. To win a hand in video poker, it must simply match one of the hands defined on the posted payout schedule. You don't have to beat anyone.

Another important point is that the rank of a winning combination is usually immaterial. That is, three kings pay the same as three deuces, and an aces-up two pair pays the same as any other two pair. And finally, you can't fold your hand, so you must draw no matter how bad a hand you were dealt.

Many players who have never seen any video poker strategy information continue to apply their own draw poker strategy. They do things such as keeping an ace or face-card kicker when drawing to a pair. This fools nobody (there aren't any other players to fool) and, although it doesn't change the probability of drawing another pair, it greatly reduces the odds of drawing three-of-a-kind, four-of-a-kind, or a full house. In other words: Never keep a kicker.

In the table game a player would normally drop out rather than draw four cards to a single face card. Since dropping is not an option in video poker, holding one face card is frequently done in a jacks-or-better game. For a garbage hand that doesn't even have a low pair or a face card, it is appropriate to draw five new cards. These situations are all covered in the playing strategy tables.

VIDEO POKER – THE GAME

As with slot machines, to activate a video poker machine you must feed it money. Do this by sliding a greenback into a slot or by dropping in one or more coins. A one dollar bill will give you four credits on a quarter machine or twenty credits on a nickel machine, which you can then play in any desired amount, usually up to a maximum of five. While inserting a bill will simply register an appropriate number of credits, dropping in one or more coins will actually start the machine. If you insert five coins or press the PLAY 5 CREDITS button, the machine will deal your initial hand automatically. The following button arrangement is typical, although most of the newer machines now also use touch screens.

CASH OUT	BET ONE CREDIT	HOLD – CANCEL	HOLD – CANCEL	HOLD – CANCEL	HOLD – CANCEL	HOLD – CANCEL	PLAY FIVE CREDITS	DEAL – DRAW

If you insert fewer than five coins or enter fewer than five credits, you will have to press DEAL or DEAL–DRAW to see your initial hand. The machine will then display five cards on the video screen, which constitute your starting hand.

Now, examine the hand carefully to decide which cards you want to save or discard. Do this by pressing the appropriate HOLD or HOLD–CANCEL buttons, which are approximately lined up with the cards on the video screen. On machines with touch-sensitive screens, you can just touch the screen images of the cards that you want to keep.

You may hold or discard any number of cards you wish. If you change your mind, press any of the HOLD buttons (or touch the screen) again and the action will be reversed. Sometimes the HOLD buttons don't register correctly, so you should check to see that the word HELD appears by each card you intend to keep. Note that, instead of HOLD buttons, some older machines may have DISCARD buttons, which act the reverse of HOLD buttons.

Should you be so fortunate to be dealt a pat hand, you must be careful not to inadvertently discard any of the cards. Although a few machines have a STAND or HOLD ALL button, on most you have to press all five HOLD buttons. Be certain all five cards in your hand display the word "HELD" before you press DRAW. If you accidentally hold or discard the wrong card, don't feel stupid—we all do it sooner or later. It usually happens when you are tired or are playing too fast.

When you are ready to draw, press DRAW or DEAL–DRAW and every card that is not held will be replaced with a new card. This is your final hand. If it matches one of the payout combinations, the machine will automatically register the appropriate number of credits. The payout table is located on either a glass panel above the screen or on the video screen itself.

With some modifications, the payout schedule is based on standard poker hands. In games without wild cards, the minimum payout is usually for a pair of jacks (jacks or better) although there are some machines that set the minimum at a pair of tens, a pair of kings, or two pair. For games with deuces wild, the minimum payout is for three-of-a-kind. Many games also pay bonuses for four-of-a-kinds of a specific rank or royal flushes with the cards in a specific order.

When you are finished playing, pressing the CASH OUT button converts the credits on the machine to coins that will be dropped into the coin tray with a loud clatter. On the newer machines you won't hear a clatter—you'll just get a cash ticket. You may also press this button anytime between hands. Don't ever forget to press the CASH OUT button when you leave the machine, or someone else will do it for you.

VIDEO POKER – THE MACHINE

Externally, video poker machines appear to come in a great variety of types, styles, and flavors. Internally, however, they are all quite similar. Each one contains a specialized microprocessor, along with its memory and support chips that control every aspect of the machine's operation. The major difference between machines is how the microprocessor is programmed.

Whenever a new hand is about to be dealt, the machine shuffles the deck electronically. To ensure that the shuffle is done honestly, the poker program in each machine accesses a constantly-running random number generator to assure that the fifty-two cards (fifty-three cards with a joker) in the deck are always dealt out in a random fashion. Fundamentally, the RNG is a program algorithm within the machine's microprocessor that continually generates pseudo-random numbers. To further assure complete randomness, the RNG randomly accesses over a billion different number sequences and typically cycles through them at a rate of more than one thousand per second. Thus, there is no chance that the player can affect the randomness of the deal.

It is the programming of the RNG that is of greatest concern to state gaming regulators whenever a new model machine is being evaluated. They examine the mathematical basis for the algorithm and verify, by testing, that the machine consistently deals random hands. If the deal is random, and the machine payouts are in accordance with its posted schedule, then the player cannot be cheated. As a result, in states that have effective gaming controls (such as Nevada and New Jersey), the chance of encountering a rigged machine is almost nonexistent. Unless you are playing in an illegal or uncontrolled gambling hall, don't worry about it.

Once the initial hand is dealt by the machine, it waits for the player to decide which cards to discard. The replacement draw cards are then sequentially dealt out from the random deck for each discarded card when the player presses the DRAW button. The machine then indicates whether or not the final hand is a winner.

VIDEO POKER HANDS

Although the winning hands in video poker are similar to standard table poker, there are some deviations. For instance, in a table poker game with wild cards, five-of-a-kind is the highest-value hand. In the vast majority of wild-card video poker games, however, five-of-a-kind is a lower value hand than a royal flush. Following are the most common paying hands in video poker, along with the approximate odds of making the hand after the draw:

Royal Flush

This is an ace-high straight flush with no wild cards. Also called a natural royal. For most payout schedules, a royal flush will occur once in 40,000 to 45,000 hands, or a little more often if you sacrifice pat hands to draw to a royal. The cards may appear on the video screen in any order, as below.

Don't be discouraged if you can't seem to get a royal flush; at 40,000 to 1, it can be a long time in coming. One day at the Plaza, a lady sitting next to me hit a royal flush, so I glibly muttered, "Guess this is your lucky day." She turned to me and snapped, "And it's about time!"

Sequential Royal

This is a royal flush in which the five cards must appear in ordered sequence on the video screen, as below.

Some machines require the sequence to be right-to-left, that is, with the ten at the right end and the ace at the left end. Using perfect playing strategy, you will make a sequential royal an average of once in four to five million hands, so don't hold your breath. An even tougher variation is when the sequential royal has to be in a specific suit, which multiplies the odds by four.

Reversible Royal

Same as the sequential royal except that the sequence can be in either direction, reducing the odds to one in two-plus million. Don't hold your breath for this one, either.

Suited Royal

A royal flush of a particular designated suit. If you don't change strategy, this hand occurs one-quarter as often as a regular royal flush, or about once in every 160,000 hands. If the strategy favors the specified suit, then it occurs a little more often.

Joker Royal or Deuce Royal

A royal flush with wild cards. In a joker-wild game, the odds of making it are about one in 12,000. In a deuces-wild game, the odds are about one in 600. The cards may appear on the video screen in any order, as below.

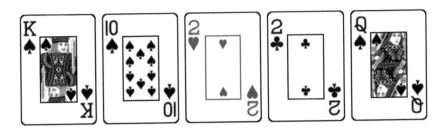

Five-of-a-Kind

Five cards of the same rank. Since a standard deck has only four cards of a given rank, one of each suit, this hand necessarily includes at least one wild card.

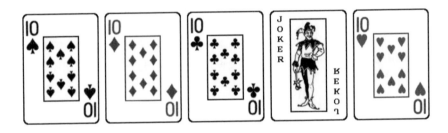

In some joker-wild games, this is the top-paying hand and will occur once in about 11,000 hands; in deuces wild, the odds are one in 300 hands. In deuces and joker wild games, the top-paying hand is five wild cards, which occurs about once in 130,000 hands.

Straight Flush

Five consecutive cards, all of the same suit. When the ace is part of the sequence, it is always low because if it is high, the result is a royal flush. A natural straight flush is typically made about once in 9,000 hands. This improves to once in 1700 hands with a joker, and once in 200 hands with deuces wild.

Four-of-a-Kind

Four cards of the same rank, also called quads. The fifth card is unrelated. Quads can be made an average of about once in every 425 hands. In joker poker, the odds drop to one in 120, and the four wild cards in deuces wild drop the odds to once in every 16 hands.

Since quads is a pat hand in a jacks-or-better game, the conventional wisdom is not to draw the fifth card since there is no way to improve the hand. However, in video poker not drawing a card to four-of-a-kind is a bad habit to get into. If you play both wildcard and jacks-or-better games you might, without thinking, not draw when you are playing with wild cards and miss a potential five-of-a-kind.

Four-of-a-Kind (Aces)

When four-of-a-kind is limited to a single specified rank, it is usually aces, but may also be kings, queens, or deuces. A high payout for four deuces is typically found in deuces wild games. The odds of making four-of-a-kind of a specified rank are one in 5,000.

Four-of-a-Kind (Faces)

When four-of-a-kind is limited to three specified ranks, it is often the face cards (jacks, queens, and kings), but more often twos, threes, and fours, as a group. The odds are about one in 2,000.

Full House

Three-of-a-kind and a pair. With no wild cards, a full house occurs once in every ninety hands. In joker poker, the odds are one in 65, and in deuces wild, the odds are one in 40.

Flush

Five cards of the same suit. This hand is made as often as a full house—once in every ninety hands. Joker poker is one in 65, and deuces wild is one in 60.

Straight

Five consecutive cards of mixed suits. Straights occur about as often as full houses and flushes in non-wild and joker poker games.

In deuces wild, however, the chances of making a straight improves dramatically to one in 18.

Three-of-a-Kind

Three cards of the same rank. The remaining two cards are unrelated. The chances of ending up with trips is about one in fourteen hands. In joker poker, it is one in eight, and in deuces wild, it is one in four. Three-of-a-kind is the lowest-paying hand in deuces wild.

Two Pair

A pair of one rank and a pair of another rank. The fifth card is unrelated. Two pair wins one out of eight hands in non-wild and joker poker games. This is not a paying hand in deuces wild, and is the lowest-paying hand in many joker poker schedules.

Jacks or Better

Two cards of the same rank. They must be either jacks, queens, kings, or aces. The three remaining cards are unrelated. A pair of jacks or better wins about every five hands. In non-wild games, this is usually the lowest-paying hand. In some games, however, the lowest paying hand may be tens or better, kings or better, or a pair of aces.

FINDING THE BEST VIDEO POKER MACHINE

THE HOUSE PERCENTAGE

The average amount of money that a video poker machine returns to the player after a long period of play is called the payback. The payback is usually stated as a percentage of the amount that the player invested in the machine. If, for example, the payback of a game is 98 percent, then, over the long term, you can expect to sustain a 2 percent loss on each hand.

The payback of the game also determines the average profit made by the casino, which is called the house percentage. For a payback of 98 percent, every $100 put into the machine will return a long-term average of $98 to the player. The remaining $2 is the casino's profit. Actually, the $98 is an expectation. It could be more and it could be less. It is the amount that, statistically speaking, is expected to be returned in the form of winnings over a very long period of time. Over the short term, however, anything can happen.

For any given machine, there are two payback numbers. One is the maximum payback for perfect play. This is the payback of interest to the player. It is the highest possible return when the best playing strategy is used, and is the one I have in mind whenever the term "payback" is used in this chapter. To the casino, this payback has only academic interest because it does not directly define the casino's profit.

The other payback is based on the actual recorded return from the machine. It is the one that the casino cares about because it is an estimate of the casino's potential long-term profit on that machine. Since many players do not apply the best strategy or bet the maximum coins, the payback for those players is typically 2 percent to 4 percent lower than for perfect play. Thus, if the maximum attainable payback on a machine is 98 percent, the actual recorded payback will typically be 95 to 96 percent, leaving the casino with a 4 to 5 percent profit.

COIN MULTIPLIERS

All video poker machines employ coin/credit multipliers. Most machines will accept one through five coins (or credits) for each hand played. The more coins deposited, the higher the payout for each winning hand. The payouts increase proportionately to the number of coins or credits, except that the largest jackpot is significantly higher when five coins are played. Coin multipliers are designed to encourage players to bet the maximum number of coins.

For most winning hands, the payout for five coins is five times the payout for one coin. For the top hand, however, the jackpot payout for five coins is typically sixteen to twenty times the payout for one coin. For example, the payout for a royal flush is typically 250 coins or credits for each coin or credit played. Thus, for two coins played, you would win 500 coins; for three coins, you would win 750; and for four coins, you would win 1000. For five coins, however, instead of winning 1250 coins, you would win 4000 coins. On some machines, you would win 4700 or 5000 coins.

As a result, when fewer than the maximum number of coins is bet, the average long-term payback percentage is reduced by 1 to 2 percent. For this reason, the strategies presented in this chapter are based on five-coin play. The only exception is for the Second Chance machines described below.

DETAILS OF THE GAMES

Even within a single casino, there can be a bewildering array of different kinds of video poker machines. One way to sort them out is to group them into major categories. Many players come to prefer certain types of machines, which is fine so long as they seek out the best paying machines within that type. Although new kinds of video poker machines regularly appear in the casinos, the following are the major ones to be found today:

NON-PROGRESSIVE MACHINES

Jacks or Better

This was the original form of video poker and is still very popular today. The lowest paying hand is a pair of jacks, and there are no wild cards. The payout schedule is based on standard poker hands and, except for a royal flush, the ranks of the cards in a given hand are immaterial. That is, four deuces are worth the same as four queens, and a king-high straight is worth the same as a five-high straight. These machines come in a variety of paybacks from fair (95 to 96 percent) to good (97 to 98 percent) to excellent (99 to 100 percent).

Two Pair or Better

The name tells the tale. The lowest paying hand is two pair. The best of these machines has a pretty good payback of 98 percent, but there are also versions that pay only 94 percent. You will often find two-pairs machines scattered among the jacks-or-better machines; the casinos take advantage of the fact that some players don't seem to know the difference.

Bonus Quads

Bonus machines are basically jacks-or-better machines that offer bonus payouts for specified four-of-a-kind (quad) hands. These non-progressive machines, including double, double-double, and triple bonus varieties, have extra-high payouts for certain quads such as four aces, four face cards, four eights, etc. To compensate for these bonuses, the payouts on some standard hands are somewhat reduced and, in one case, the lowest payout is changed from jacks-or-better to kings-or-better. As a group, these are the best paying machines in Nevada with paybacks in the range of 98 to 100 percent. As a result, they have become the most popular types of video poker machines around. The versions found in Atlantic City and along the Mississippi, however, only pay about 94 to 98 percent.

Bonus Royals

This is a small category of non-progressive bonus machines that, instead of quads, have extra-high payouts for certain royal flushes. Most of these games pay back in the range of 98 to 100 percent, but depend on some jackpot combinations that occur very rarely, such as a sequential royal flush.

Joker Wild

This game uses a fifty-three-card deck in which the joker is a wild card. The joker can be substituted for any other card in the deck. In most cases, a royal flush with a joker (called a joker royal) does not pay as well as a natural. Many players are attracted to joker poker, despite the fact that in many versions of the game the payback is only fair. Although there have been a few machines out there that pay as high as 101 percent, most of them pay in the range of 94 to 97 percent.

Deuces Wild

As the name suggests, in this game the four deuces are wild cards. In all cases, a royal flush with deuces (called a deuce royal) pays much less than a natural because it is (typically) eighty times easier to make. All other hands, however, pay the same with or without deuces. Although the lowest-paying hand is three-of-a-kind, many versions of deuces wild have an excellent payback of 98 to 101 percent. However, be careful; there are some that pay only 94 to 96 percent.

Deuces and Joker Wild

Five wild cards in a fifty-three-card deck result in a very lively game with over half the hands being potential winners, although they are mostly pushes. If you can find one, the deuces and joker wild machines have an excellent 99 percent payback in Nevada casinos, but the versions found along the Mississippi pay only about 93 percent.

Double Joker

Two wild jokers in a fifty-four-card deck, with two pair being the lowest-paying hand. So far, this game has only been available in Atlantic City. There are two almost identical versions: one has an excellent payback of 100 percent, while the other pays less than 98 percent.

PROGRESSIVE MACHINES

A progressive jackpot network is a group of machines that are electrically connected to a common jackpot pool. As people play the machines, a small percentage of the money paid in by the players is diverted to the jackpot pool, which continues to grow until someone wins it. The jackpot is then reset to a predetermined minimum value and the growth cycle repeats itself. Each player is competing against the other players on that network, and each time coins are inserted, the jackpot gets a little larger.

A progressive network may consist of a bank of a dozen machines with a jackpot that rarely exceeds a few thousand dollars. The winning progressive hand is usually a natural royal flush, so the chance of hitting the jackpot in such a small, localized network is not unreasonable. Local banks of progressive machines can be found for many varieties of games including original jacks or better, bonus quads, bonus royals, deuces wild, and joker wild.

If the machine is part of a city-wide or state-wide network that interconnects hundreds of other machines, the winning progressive hand is always a very rare combination such as a sequential royal flush. Consequently, the jackpot pool can reach lifestyle-altering levels. The chance of winning that jackpot is almost as small as the chance of winning the Power Ball lottery.

Many progressive players do not care about the overall payback of the machine, since they are only interested in the main jackpot. Until the jackpot gets quite high, the long-term payback for wide-area network games is only fair—and the short-term payback is never very good.

DOUBLE DOWN STUD

Double-down stud is not another version of draw poker, but is loosely based on the game of five-card stud poker. Since double-down stud requires little skill and has a simple playing strategy, it will be fully covered in this section. This game has not really caught on, probably because the long-term average payback is less than 98 percent.

You begin playing by inserting one to ten coins—the tenth coin doubles the payout for a royal flush. Four cards are dealt face up, and you are given the option of doubling your original bet before the fifth card is dealt. When you make your choice, the fifth card is exposed and the machine pays in accordance with the following chart:

DOUBLE DOWN STUD - FIFTH CARD PAYOUT SCHEDULE		
Winning Hand	1 coin	10 coins
Royal Flush	1000	20,000
Straight Flush	200	2000
4 of a Kind	50	500
Full House	12	120
Flush	9	90
Straight	6	60
3 of a Kind	4	40
Two Pair	3	30
Pair of: J, Q, K, or A	2	20
Pair of: 6, 7, 8, 9, or 10	1	10

If you insert ten coins, the payout for a royal flush is increased to two thousand per coin. The best playing strategy is to double when you have the following situations:

- Any paying hand, from a pair of sixes on up.
- A possible royal flush.
- A possible straight flush.
- A possible flush.
- A possible straight (open-ended).

Do not double on a pair smaller than a six. Do not double an inside or single-ended straight. Remember, this is not draw poker so you do not get to discard any unwanted cards. You just get to see the fifth card after making the doubling decision. This game is only described here in the interest of completeness. It is not recommended, but you may want to try it as a diversion from the draw poker games.

NOVELTIES AND ODDITIES

Many video poker machines contain stratagems to help you lose your money a little faster. Some of these ploys kick in after your final hand is displayed and give you another opportunity to win or to lose what you have already won. Although most of them have no effect on the basic playing strategy, each one will be described so you can decide whether or not you want to play along.

Multi-Hand

The first multi-hand video poker game, called Triple Play, is an interesting variant in that it isn't quite what it appears to be. The player is dealt three hands at once from three different decks, but only one hand is exposed. The exposed hand is played in a normal manner and when the draw occurs, the same cards that were held appear in the other two hands. Each of the three hands then gets replacement cards dealt from its respective deck. Thus, if you start off with a good hand, you will have three good hands, but if you have a bad hand, you will have three bad hands.

From the standpoint of mathematical probability, this is exactly like playing three different machines simultaneously. The fact that the three hands always have the same held cards somehow adds an exciting flavor. This is often a multi-game machine from which the player may select one of several standard versions of bonus quads or deuces wild. To get all three hands dealt, at least three coins or three credits must be played. To qualify for the maximum jackpot payout, however, fifteen coins (or credits) must be played—five for each hand. This accounts for the popularity of the nickel version.

There are now four-, ten-, fifty-, and one hundred-hand machines available. You can play any number of hands on any of them, but even on the penny version of the one hundred-hand machine, to qualify for the maximum jackpot on all hands costs $5. Of course, if you play only a single hand in any of these games, it acts like a normal video poker machine.

Double or Nothing

On a few video poker machines, whenever you get a winning hand, you are given the option of risking the entire payout on a double-or-nothing bet. If you press the YES button, five new cards appear on the screen, four down and one up. You may then select one of the four face-down cards. If it is higher than the first face-up card, the payout is doubled; if it is lower, you lose your winnings, and the game is concluded. A tie is a push, and is replayed. You may continue the doubling-up game as many times as you wish—until you lose.

Although this turns out to be a very fair even-money proposition, it is not recommended. Statistically, the probability of losing is cumulative, so that if you try to double more than one time in succession, your overall chances of winning rapidly decrease. On the first try, the chance of winning is 50 percent, on the second, it is 25 percent, on the third, it is 12.5 percent, and so on. Like any repeated double-or-nothing proposition, you will eventually lose your money.

Double Card

Some jacks-or-better video poker machines deal from a fifty-three-card deck where the extra card is a doubling card. No, it is not a wild card. When it appears in a winning hand, it doubles the payout. Although at first glance it seems like a good deal, whenever the double card appears, it effectively reduces your five-card hand to a four-card hand. The doubling card actually interferes with any winning hand that requires five cards such as a straight, flush, or royal flush. If you get a four-straight or a four-flush and the fifth card is a double, you should discard the double. Better yet, you should discard this game.

Second Chance

On some video poker machines, you are given the option of taking a sixth card whenever your final hand, after the draw, is one that could be improved to a straight or better. The sixth card is dealt from the remaining cards in the same randomly shuffled deck that was used for the original hand. A new payout schedule appears on the screen showing the possible winning hands for that particular situation. For instance, if your final hand is two pair, the new schedule will show a payout for a possible full house. This payout is not necessarily the same as the original payout schedule, but is set so that the overall payback with the sixth card is about 97 percent, which is usually less than the overall payback of the machine.

If, after the draw, you have a possible straight or better, the back of a sixth card will appear on the screen and the SECOND CHANCE button will illuminate. To accept the option, press the button. You may now insert one to five additional coins (or credits), regardless of how many coins you originally bet. The machine will expose the sixth card and automatically select the best five out of the six cards

The main advantage to second chance is that you can change the value of your bet in midstream. Therefore, the best initial approach is to play one coin at a time and use the recommended strategy for the posted payout schedule. Only activate the second chance option if you draw four cards to a royal. Then insert five coins (or credits) to maximize the jackpot and go for the sixth card.

Progressive Second Chance

This is another version of second chance that has a separate progressive jackpot for royal flushes. The option kicks in when you have four cards to a royal flush. It can raise the overall payback of the machine to well over 100 percent, even when the jackpot is at its lowest level. You are allowed to drop in five coins, even if your original bet was only a single coin. Be sure to do that. Progressive Second Chance is definitely a worthwhile gamble.

VIDEO POKER STRATEGY

After the initial five cards are dealt out, it is up to the player to decide which cards to hold and which to discard. This decision is the only control exercised by the player and is a significant factor in the outcome of the game. Therefore, it is important to apply the correct playing strategy when making the hold/discard decision.

There are many good descriptions of the perfect mathematical strategy for drawing cards in video poker, but most of them over-complicate the problem. For instance, a portion of the strategy for jacks-or-better is often given as:

JACKS OR BETTER STRATEGY	
4-Card Outside Straight Flush	Draw 1 card
Two Pair	Draw 1 card
4-Card Inside Straight Flush	Draw 1 card

What this means is that drawing to an outside straight flush is preferential to drawing to two pair, and that drawing to two pair is preferential to drawing to an inside straight flush. This strategy is absolutely correct. However, a possible straight flush and two pairs cannot occur in the same hand, so the strategy can be simplified by saying:

SIMPLIFIED JACKS OR BETTER STRATEGY	
4-Card Straight Flush	Draw 1 card
Two Pair	Draw 1 card

This is mathematically identical to the more complicated version. In fact, one can also say:

SIMPLIFIED JACKS OR BETTER STRATEGY	
Two Pair	Draw 1 card
4-Card Straight Flush	Draw 1 card

without fear of contradiction. Since both hands are mutually exclusive, it doesn't matter in what order they are listed in the strategy table. This is typical of the simplifications used in this section.

Simplification was sometimes attained by rounding to the second decimal place in the probability calculations for some of the dealt hands. When compared with most published strategies that are based on very precise numbers, the difference in real-world play turns out to be negligible.

To apply the mathematical strategy with absolute accuracy takes considerable concentration, which is simply not possible for most people. With all the distractions in a typical casino, trying to use a complicated strategy can easily result in inadvertent playing errors that reduce the overall payback. The simplified strategy presented here will reduce such errors and result in coming closer to the maximum theoretical payback for the machine being played.

BASIC STRATEGY RULES

To assure that you are getting the highest return from a video poker machine, a certain amount of playing discipline must be used. The following basic rules have to be followed to assure that the best strategy is effectively applied:

Play the Maximum Coins

Last year, while waiting for somebody, I was killing time by idly playing a jacks-or-better machine, one quarter at a time. When my friend showed up, the machine had five credits left, so I hit the PLAY 5 CREDITS button, just to be done with it. To my amazement, I was dealt three high spades and made the royal on the draw. The payout was four thousand coins ($1000), or the equivalent of eight hundred coins per quarter. Had I continued to play one quarter at a time, the payout would have been only 250 coins, or a measly $62.50. The moral to this story is to play the maximum coins (usually five), unless you have a very good reason not to.

The one consistency in all video poker machines is that the per-coin payout for the highest hand is always enhanced when the maximum number of coins (or credits) is played. Although there are situations where single-coin play is advisable (such as Second Chance machines), the following playing strategies are based on five-coin play, unless otherwise noted.

Many recreational players find that dollar machines deplete their bankroll too quickly. Therefore, if you feel uneasy playing for $5 a hand, move to a quarter machine. If you insist on playing fewer than the maximum coins, be aware that the long-term payback will be reduced by 1 to 2 percent—and much more if you hit an early royal, as I did. However, there is one caution: if you move from a quarter machine to a nickel machine, be sure that the payout schedule is the same. Although there isn't much variation in schedules between quarter, dollar, and five-dollar machines, most nickel machines have significantly poorer payout schedules.

Never Hold a Kicker

A kicker is an unmatched card held in the hand when drawing replacement cards. Some video poker players hate to discard an ace, even if keeping it doesn't improve their hand. This is a throwback to the table game where such strategy is sometimes appropriate. In video poker, however, holding a kicker is disastrous because it significantly reduces the chances of improving a hand. For instance, on a full-pay jacks-or-better machine, keeping a kicker with a high pair reduces the overall payback by over 1.5 percent. If you are dealt a low pair, discarding two instead of three cards reduces the payback by almost 4 percent. Don't do it.

Stick to the Strategy

Do not try to outguess the strategy table. The table is based on mathematical probabilities and your hunch is not. Occasionally you may guess correctly, but over the long run, the strategy table will serve you well. If you don't like the idea of breaking a straight or a flush in order to draw one card to a possible royal, maybe you are playing the wrong game.

Do Not Depend on Your Memory

Take this book or copies of the strategy tables into the casino and refer to them frequently. Until you are familiar with a particular version of video poker, don't depend too much on your memory. After you have played a particular game for a while, you will get to know the strategy by heart.

PAYOUT SCHEDULES AND STRATEGY TABLES

The following sections provide payout schedules and strategy tables for six basic varieties of video poker. These are:

SIX VARIETIES OF VIDEO POKER
Jacks or Better
Bonus and Double Bonus Poker
Double Double and Triple Bonus Poker
Deuces Wild
Joker Poker – Kings or Better
Joker Poker – Two Pair

Selecting the Best Machine

In each section, a selection of abbreviated payout schedules is shown for that type of game, which is followed by the strategy table. The house edge is given for each payout schedule so that you can decide if that is a game you want to play. Following is an example of a complete payout schedule.

JACKS OR BETTER					
Credits Bet	1	2	3	4	5
Royal Flush	250	500	750	1000	4000
Straight Flush	50	100	150	200	250
Four of a Kind	25	50	75	100	125
Full House	9	18	27	36	45
Flush	6	12	18	24	30
Straight	4	8	12	16	20
Three of a Kind	3	6	9	12	15
Two Pair	2	4	6	8	10
Jacks or Better	1	2	3	4	5

To save space and make comparisons easier, the schedules shown in the following sections show only the one-credit columns. These are the columns you should examine and compare when selecting your machine. Except for the five-credit royal flush payout, the other columns are simply multiples of the one-credit column. The payback percentages given are for perfect strategy and five-credit play.

Applying the Playing Strategy

After selecting your machine, turn the page to the strategy table for that type of game. The strategy table lists all possible hands in the order they should be played. After the initial five cards are dealt, work your way down from the top of the strategy table until you find a match and then draw the indicated number of cards.

You do not have to consult the strategy table for every hand that is dealt. For most hands, the correct strategy is obvious. The main purpose of the table is to resolve conflicts when there is more than one way to logically play a hand. For instance, what do you do if you are dealt a pat flush that includes a four-card royal? What about a four-flush that includes a three-card royal? And once you have learned these things, remember to recheck the strategy table whenever you play a new type of game.

Jacks or Better

JACKS OR BETTER – PAYOUT SCHEDULES				
Royal Flush	250	250	250	250	250
Straight Flush	50	50	200	40	50
4 of a Kind	25	80	30	20	80
Full House	9	8	8	9	8
Flush	6	6	8	6	5
Straight	4	4	8	4	4
3 of a Kind	3	3	3	3	3
2 Pair	2	1	1	2	1
Jacks or Better	1	1	1	1	1
Payback	99.5%	98.5%	98.5%	98.3%	97.4%

Royal Flush	250	250	250	250	250
Straight Flush	50	50	50	50	50
4 of a Kind	25	80	25	20	25
Full House	8	7	7	7	6
Flush	5	5	5	5	5
Straight	4	4	4	4	4
3 of a Kind	3	3	3	3	3
2 Pair	2	1	2	2	2
Jacks or Better	1	1	1	1	1
Payback	97.3%	96.3%	96.2%	95.5%	95.0%

The paybacks shown on the previous page are for schedules with a Royal Flush five-credit payout of four thousand credits. For schedules paying 4,700 credits, increase the payback by 0.3 percent. For five thousand credits, increase the payback by 0.5 percent.

JACKS OR BETTER — STRATEGY TABLE	
DEALT HAND	DRAW
Royal Flush	0
Straight Flush	0
4 of a Kind	0
Full House	0
4-Card Royal Flush	1
Flush	0
Straight	0
3 of a Kind	2
2 Pair	1
4-Card Straight Flush	1
Pair J, Q, K, or A	3
3-Card Royal Flush	2
4-Card Flush	1
Pair 2 thru 10	3
4-Card Outside Straight	1
3-Card Straight Flush	2
4-Card Inside Straight (3 or 4 HC)	1
J-A, Q-A, or K-A (same suit)	3
J-Q-K (mixed suits)	2
10-J, 10-Q, or 10-K (same suit)	3
1 or 2 High Cards	3-4
Mixed Low Cards	5

Bonus or Double Bonus Poker

BONUS OR DOUBLE BONUS POKER — PAYOUT SCHEDULES					
Royal Flush	250	250	250	250	250
Straight Flush	100	50	50	50	50
4 – Aces	200	80	80	80	160
4 – 2s, 3s, or 4s	40	40	40	40	80
4 – 5s thru Kings	25	25	25	25	50
Full House	12	8	7	6	9
Flush	8	5	5	5	6
Straight	5	4	4	4	4
3 of a Kind	3	3	3	3	3
2 Pair	1	2	2	2	1
Jacks or Better	1	1	1	1	1
Payback	99.4%	99.2%	98.0%	96.9%	96.5%

Royal Flush	250	250	250	250	250
Straight Flush	50	50	50	50	50
4 – Aces	160	160	160	160	160
4 – 2s, 3s, or 4s	80	80	80	80	80
4 – 5s thru Kings	50	50	50	50	50
Full House	10	9	9	9	9
Flush	7	7	6	7	6
Straight	5	5	5	4	4
3 of a Kind	3	3	3	3	3
2 Pair	1	1	1	1	1
Jacks or Better	1	1	1	1	1
Payback	100.2%	99.1%	97.8%	97.7%	96.5%

The paybacks shown above are for schedules with a Royal Flush five-credit payout of four thousand credits.

BONUS OR DOUBLE BONUS POKER — STRATEGY TABLE	
DEALT HAND	DRAW
Royal Flush	0
Straight Flush	0
4 of a Kind	0
Full House	0
4-Card Royal Flush	1
Flush	0
Straight	0
3 of a Kind	2
2 Pair	1
4-Card Straight Flush	1
Pair J, Q, K, or A	3
3-Card Royal Flush	2
4-Card Flush	1
Pair 2 thru 10	3
4-Cd Outside Straight (1 to 3 HC)	1
9-10-J (same suit)	2
4-Card Outside Straight	1
3-Card Straight Flush	2
J-Q-K-A (mixed suits)	1
2-Card Royal Flush	3
J-Q-K (mixed suits)	2
1 or 2 High Cards	3-4
Mixed Low Cards	5

Double Double or Triple Bonus Poker

DOUBLE DOUBLE OR TRIPLE BONUS POKER — PAYOUT SCHEDULES					
Royal Flush	250	250	250	250	250
Straight Flush	80	60	100	80	50
4 – Aces	240	400	240	240	240
4 – 2s, 3s, or 4s	120	80	120	120	120
4 – 5s thru Kings	50	50	50	50	75
Full House	9	7	8	8	10
Flush	5	5	5	5	7
Straight	4	4	4	4	4
3 of a Kind	3	3	3	3	3
2 Pair	1	1	1	1	1
Jacks or Better	1	1	1	1	1
Payback	99.6%	98.9%	98.7%	98.5%	98.5%

Royal Flush	250	250	250	250	250
Straight Flush	50	50	50	50	50
4 – Aces w/ 2,3,4	400	400	400	400	400
4 – 2,3,or 4 w/ A,2,3,4	160	160	160	160	160
4 – Aces	160	160	160	160	160
4 – 2s ,3s, or 4s	80	80	80	80	80
4 – 5s thru Kings	50	50	50	50	50
Full House	10	9	9	8	6
Flush	6	6	5	5	5
Straight	4	4	4	4	4
3 of a Kind	3	3	3	3	3
2 Pair	1	1	1	1	1
Jacks or Better	1	1	1	1	1
Payback	100.1%	99.0%	97.9%	96.8%	94.7%

The paybacks shown on the preceding page are for schedules with a Royal Flush five-credit payout of four thousand credits.

DOUBLE DOUBLE OR TRIPLE BONUS POKER — STRATEGY TABLE	
DEALT HAND	DRAW
Royal Flush	0
Straight Flush	0
4 of a Kind	0
3 Aces	2
4-Card Royal Flush	1
Flush	0
Straight	0
Full House	0
3 of a Kind	2
4-Card Outside Straight Flush	1
Pair Aces	3
4-Card Inside Straight Flush	1
2 Pairs	1
Pair J, Q, or K	3
3-Card Royal Flush	2
4-Card Flush	1
4-Card Outside Straight	1
Pair 2 thru 10	3
9-10-J (same suit)	2
J-Q-K-A (mixed suits)	1
3-Card Straight Flush	2
2-Card Royal Flush	3
J-Q-K (mixed suits)	2

(continued next page)

DOUBLE DOUBLE OR TRIPLE BONUS POKER — STRATEGY TABLE *(continued)*	
DEALT HAND	DRAW
1 Ace	4
4-Card Inside Straight	1
1 or 2 High Cards	3-4
Mixed Low Cards	5

Deuces Wild

DEUCES WILD — PAYOUT SCHEDULES					
Natural Royal	250	250	250	250	250
4 – Deuces	200	500	200	400	500
Deuce Royal	25	25	25	25	25
5 of a Kind	15	15	16	16	12
Straight Flush	9	8	10	11	8
4 of a Kind	5	4	4	4	4
Full House	3	3	4	3	3
Flush	2	2	3	2	2
Straight	2	2	2	2	2
3 of a Kind	1	1	1	1	1
Payback	100.7%	100.2%	99.7%	99.6%	99.2%

Natural Royal	250	250	250	250	250
4 – Deuces	500	200	200	200	200
Deuce Royal	25	20	25	20	20
5 of a Kind	15	12	15	15	12
Straight Flush	5	9	9	9	9
4 of a Kind	4	5	4	4	4
Full House	3	3	4	4	4
Flush	2	2	3	3	3
Straight	2	2	2	2	2
3 of a Kind	1	1	1	1	1
Payback	99.1%	98.9%	98.9%	98.0%	97.1%

The paybacks shown above are for schedules with a Royal Flush five-credit payout of four thousand credits.

DEUCES WILD — STRATEGY TABLE	
NO DEUCES	**DRAW**
Natural Royal Flush	0
4-Card Royal Flush	1
Straight Flush	0
4 of a Kind	1
Full House, Flush, or Straight	0
3 of a Kind	2
4-Card Straight Flush	1
3-Card Royal Flush	2
3-Card Outside Straight Flush	2
1 Pair (discard 2nd pair)	3
4-Card Outside Straight	1
4-Card Flush	1
3-Card Inside Straight Flush	2
2-Card Royal Flush	3
Assorted Cards	5
ONE DEUCE HAND	**DRAW**
Royal Flush or 5 of a Kind	0
Straight Flush	0
4 of a Kind	1
4-Card Royal Flush	1
4-Card Straight Flush	1
Full House, Flush or Straight	0
3 of a Kind	2
3-Card Royal Flush	2
3-Card Straight Flush	2
1 Deuce	4

DEUCES WILD — STRATEGY TABLE	
TWO DEUCE HAND	**DRAW**
Royal Flush or 5 of a Kind	0
Straight Flush	0
4 of a Kind	1
4-Card Royal Flush	1
2 Deuces	3
THREE DEUCE HAND	**DRAW**
Royal Flush or 5 of a Kind	0
3 Deuces	2
FOUR DEUCE HAND	**DRAW**
4 Deuces	1

Joker Poker (Kings or Better)

JOKER POKER (KINGS OR BETTER) — PAYOUT SCHEDULES				
Natural Royal	400	400	400	400
5 of a Kind	200	200	200	200
Joker Royal	100	100	100	100
Straight Flush	50	50	50	50
4 of a Kind	20	20	17	15
Full House	7	6	7	8
Flush	5	5	5	5
Straight	3	3	3	3
3 of a Kind	2	2	2	2
2 pair	1	1	1	1
Kings or Better	1	1	1	1
Payback	100.7%	99.1%	98.1%	98.0%

Natural Royal	400	400	400	400
5 of a Kind	200	200	200	200
Joker Royal	100	100	100	100
Straight Flush	50	50	50	40
4 of a Kind	20	15	20	20
Full House	6	7	5	5
Flush	4	5	4	4
Straight	3	3	3	3
3 of a Kind	2	2	2	2
2 Pair	1	1	1	1
Kings or Better	1	1	1	1
Payback	97.6%	96.3%	96.0%	95.5%

The paybacks shown above are for schedules with a Royal Flush five-credit payout of four thousand credits. For schedules paying 4700 credits, increase the payback by 0.3 percent. For five thousand credits, increase the payback by 0.5 percent.

JOKER POKER (KINGS OR BETTER) — STRATEGY TABLE	
JOKER HAND	DRAW
Royal Flush or 5 of a Kind	0
Straight Flush	0
4 of a Kind	1
4-Card Royal Flush	1
Full House or Flush	0
4-Card Straight Flush	1
3 of a Kind	2
Straight	0
4-Card Flush (1 or 2 HC)	1
3-Card Royal Flush	2
3-Card Straight Flush	2
Pair King or Ace	3
4-Card Outside Straight	1
4-Card Flush	1
Joker	4

Joker Poker (Two Pair)

JOKER POKER (TWO PAIR) – PAYOUT SCHEDULES			
Natural Royal	500	500	500	100
5 of a Kind	100	100	100	400
Joker Royal	50	50	50	100
Straight Flush	50	50	50	100
4 of a Kind	20	20	20	16
Full House	8	10	8	8
Flush	7	6	7	5
Straight	6	5	5	4
3 of a Kind	2	2	2	2
2 Pair	1	1	1	1
Payback	101.6%	99.4%	98.6%	97.2%

Natural Royal	500	500	500	100
5 of a Kind	100	100	100	400
Joker Royal	50	50	50	100
Straight Flush	50	50	50	100
4 of a Kind	20	25	20	15
Full House	8	8	8	6
Flush	6	5	6	5
Straight	5	4	4	4
3 of a Kind	2	2	2	2
2 Pair	1	1	1	1
Payback	96.4%	95.6%	93.6%	93.3%

The paybacks shown above are for schedules with a Royal Flush five-credit payout of four thousand credits. For schedules paying 4700 credits, increase the payback by 0.3 percent. For five thousand credits, increase the payback by 0.5 percent.

JOKER POKER (TWO PAIR) — STRATEGY TABLE	
NO JOKER	DRAW
Natural Royal Flush	0
Straight Flush	0
4-Card Royal Flush	1
4 of a Kind	1
Full House, Flush, or Straight	0
4-Card Straight Flush	1
3 of a Kind	2
2 Pairs	1
3-Card Royal Flush	2
4-Card Flush	1
4-Card Outside Straight	1
3-Card Straight Flush	2
1 Pair	3
4-Card Inside Straight	1
3-Card Flush	2
2-Card Royal Flush	3
3-Card Outside Straight	2
2-Card Straight Flush	3
Assorted Cards	5

(continued next page)

JOKER POKER (TWO PAIR) — STRATEGY TABLE *(continued)*	
JOKER HAND	**DRAW**
Royal Flush or 5 of a Kind	0
Straight Flush	0
4 of a Kind	1
Full House or Flush	0
4-Card Royal Flush	1
4-Card Straight Flush	1
Straight	0
3 of a Kind	2
3-Card Straight Flush	2
4-Card Flush	1
4-Card Straight	1
3-Card Outside Straight	2
Joker	4

VIDEO KENO

If you are looking for some variety in your slot play, you can always try a video keno machine. These machines have screens that are formatted very similarly to paper keno tickets and operate just like standard slot machines.

In the game of regular keno, twenty out of a total of eighty numbers are randomly selected, and the winning numbers are posted on keno flashboards throughout the casino. When you play the game, your goal is to correctly guess as many of those twenty numbers as possible. The more numbers you get right, the bigger the payoff.

In video keno, there is also a matrix of eighty numbers from which twenty are randomly chosen by the computer in the machine. Your goal is to select up to ten spots and attempt to match as many of the computer-chosen numbers as possible. The more spots you select, the higher the possible award, but if you catch fewer of the spots you picked, the payout is greatly reduced. Although there are a few nickel and dollar keno machines, the majority of the video keno machines take one to four quarters. Increasing the number of coins proportionately increases the potential payout.

HOW TO PLAY

When you start to play, be sure that you first press the ERASE or WIPE CARD button to clear the screen. You can then select the numbers you want by touching the screen with the light pen that is attached to the machine. For each selection you make, the number will shift color. You can change your mind at any time by pressing the ERASE button and starting over. In some cases, the machine has a keyboard instead of a light pen.

When you are satisfied with your picks, press the PLAY or START button and twenty random numbers begin to appear on the screen one by one as they are selected by the internal random number generator. Any of your numbers that hit change color, and the amount of your winnings are displayed and added to the credit meter. If you bet four quarters, get lucky, and catch ten out of ten spots, you can win as much as $10,000.

Whenever you are ready to cash out, press the COLLECT or CASH OUT button and your winnings will drop into the tray with a big clatter. Large winnings—usually $300 or more—are hand paid by an attendant.

HOUSE PERCENTAGE

The house edge for video keno is much lower than for regular keno, typically ranging from about 8 to 18 percent, although there are a few greedy casinos that take much more. As with standard slot machines, the nickel machines have the highest house edge and the dollar machines usually have the lowest, however, the payback does vary somewhat from casino to casino. Of course, you will want to play at those casinos that give you the best return.

The following three pay schedules are likely to be the best you can find for quarter denomination games. Note that the numbers in the charts are the number of coins/credits paid for each coin/credit wagered.

CHAPTER 18 - VIDEO KENO

SCHEDULE #1 – VIDEO KENO (25¢)										
SPOTS SELECTED	SPOTS CAUGHT									HOUSE PCT
	1	2	3	4	5	6	7	8	9	10	
1	3										25.0
2	0	15									9.8
3	0	2	46								8.4
4	0	2	5	91							8.0
5	0	0	3	12	810						8.1
6	0	0	3	4	70	1600					7.3
7	0	0	1	2	21	400	7000				7.6
8	0	0	0	2	12	98	1652	10000			7.7
9	0	0	0	1	6	44	335	4700	10000		8.0
10	0	0	0	0	5	24	142	1000	4500	10000	7.4

SCHEDULE #2 – VIDEO KENO (25¢)										
SPOTS SELECTED	SPOTS CAUGHT									HOUSE PCT
	1	2	3	4	5	6	7	8	9	10	
2	0	15									9.8
3	0	3	37								7.0
4	0	2	4	105							8.0
5	0	0	3	12	810						8.1
6	0	0	3	5	76	1200					7.8
7	0	0	1	3	18	360	7000				7.9
8	0	0	0	1	15	122	1500	8000			8.0
9	0	0	0	1	3	58	350	5000	9000		8.0
10	0	0	0	0	3	29	140	1300	5000	10000	7.9

SCHEDULE #3 – VIDEO KENO (25¢)											
SPOTS SELECTED	SPOTS CAUGHT										HOUSE PCT
	1	2	3	4	5	6	7	8	9	10	
2	0	15									9.8
3	0	2	46								8.4
4	0	2	6	77							7.9
5	0	1	3	19	260						8.0
6	0	0	2	10	71	1200					8.0
7	0	0	1	3	19	350	7000				7.7
8	0	0	1	3	13	47	500	8000			7.7
9	0	0	1	2	4	21	181	2400	9000		8.3
10	0	0	0	1	3	17	135	1300	5000	10000	7.8

Notice that schedules #2 and #3 do not allow you to select only one number. That's just fine because the house edge for a one-number pick is too high, whether playing regular keno or video keno.

PLAYING STRATEGY

To begin, you should check the payout schedule on the machine. Some games have a printed schedule posted that has information similar to the above, except that it will not show the house percentage. Most machines, however, have a second screen above the keno matrix instead of a printed schedule. On such a machine, you'll have to put in a quarter and mark one number at a time to see the payouts.

Before you start to play, compare the payout schedule on the machine to the ones shown above. If it's not one of the above, you can assume that it isn't a good payer. If you decide to play it anyway, at least be sure the top payout (ten spots selected, ten spots caught) is ten thousand coins or credits. Otherwise, the machine isn't worth playing.

CHAPTER 18 - VIDEO KENO

Be aware that video keno is a much faster game than regular keno. In the time it takes to play one regular keno game, you can easily play thirty or forty video keno games. Thus, even with a lower house edge, you will lose money at a faster rate.

MONEY MANAGEMENT

After you have won a sum of money as the result of diligent and intelligent play, you should reap the rewards that those winnings can provide. Too many gamblers win a pile just to fritter it away by losing it back to the casino or giving it to the IRS. The purpose of money management is to retain as much of that money as possible. Hopefully, the following advice will help you to avoid those money traps.

CONTROLLING YOUR BANKROLL

Before you step up to any video poker or slot machine, be sure you have first designated a specific sum of money to risk for your playing session. Otherwise, you may end up like some impromptu gamblers who, after sustaining a losing streak, continue to dig for more money in an attempt to recoup their losses. By doing this, they may eventually lose their entire bankroll during the first day of a gambling trip, and then wonder what they are going to do the rest of the time. Some will head for the nearest ATM and start using money that was never intended for gambling. That is bad news, and is a trap that you don't want to fall into.

To avoid such a situation, let's say you are on a two-day gambling junket and have allocated $1000 that you can afford to lose. Divide that bankroll into two $500 stakes, one stake for each day. Whatever you do, don't gamble away more than $500 in any single day, and stay away from the ATMs. You must be disciplined about this.

IMPORTANT NOTE:

If you can't maintain that kind of money discipline, you have a problem and should seek help. Although they would rather not, most casinos will tell you where to go or who to call to get the necessary help. If you don't do this, you can ruin your life.

If your discipline is marginal, bring only the designated $500 with you into the casino. Leave the rest of it with your wife or lock it up in the room safe. If you lose the entire $500 stake, quit gambling for the day. Go sightseeing, see a show, have dinner, but don't gamble another cent until the following day.

The next day, repeat the procedure with the second $500, but try not to lose it all this time. If you did lose your daily stake on the first day, you should carefully read the "When to Quit" section below. By dividing your allocated gambling funds into daily stakes, you are maintaining a measure of control over your bankroll. Even if you do eventually lose it all, this form of monetary discipline will assure that you can do some gambling every day, which is the reason you went on the trip in the first place.

Now that you've determined your daily bankroll allocation, you should break that stake down for your individual gambling sessions. If you have decided that you will probably hit the machines twice a day, divide that $500 daily allocation in half and don't step up to a slot with more than $250 in your pocket. If you lose that amount and don't dig for more, you will be assured of having another playing session that day—and this time you may come out ahead.

PERSONAL BETTING LIMITS

You should determine ahead of time how much you can afford to bet. Many slot games are rather volatile, which means you may lose several spins before you start winning (or vice versa). How much, then, do you need to weather the ups and downs?

As a general rule of thumb, you should have a gambling stake of one hundred times the denomination for every hour you intend to play a two-coin game. Your stake should be proportionately higher if you wager more than two coins or credits per spin. Because of the higher payback, however, a video poker player can bet five coins per hand for the same stake.

For instance, if you allocate $200 for a four-hour playing session, your betting rate is $50 per hour. The indicated betting level would then be $0.50 ($50 ÷ 100) per spin. Thus, if you are betting two coins per spin, you should stick to quarter machines.

WHEN TO QUIT

The gambler who doesn't know when to quit will never come out ahead, no matter how well he or she plays. A commonly heard piece of advice is: "Quit when you are ahead." That's good advice, except that many people misinterpret it to mean: "Quit when you are winning." No, no, no! The correct rule is:

QUIT WHEN YOU ARE AHEAD, BUT NEVER QUIT *WHILE* YOU ARE WINNING!

When you are on a hot machine, you should always stick with it and slowly increase your bet size. Of course, you never know in advance when the machine will go cold, but sooner or later, it will. When you do start losing, cut the size of your bets right down to the minimum, and if you continue to lose, quit playing.

SET A LOSS LIMIT

The best way to handle a winning streak is to set a loss limit and stick to it. When you first get ahead, quit playing when you have lost 25 percent of your total winnings because the streak is over. If you keep winning and have doubled or tripled your bankroll, reduce the loss limit to 20 percent, and then 15 percent. The more you win, the tighter the loss limit. The idea is to protect your profit.

For example, shortly after you start playing a machine with a $300 bankroll, you find that you are $200 ahead. Mentally set a stop loss at $150 of your winnings. That is, if your $200 winnings dissipate down to $150, quit playing. You are down $50, which is 25 percent of your $200 winnings, and you walk away $150 richer.

If you keep winning, however, keep resetting the loss limit. When your winnings equal or exceed double your bankroll, start reducing the loss limit percentage. At $600, your stop loss should be $480 (20 percent), and at $1000, your stop loss should be $850 (15 percent). This, of course, is just a guideline, but wherever you set your personal loss limit, stick with it.

MINIMIZING LOSSES

But what if you win a few and lose a few, and the machine is slowly grinding down your bankroll? Once you realize what is happening, take a break or at least change machines before you lose your entire daily stake. If you maintain the proper discipline, whenever you have gone through your daily gambling allotment, you are through gambling for the day.

REEL GOOD ADVICE

Whatever you do, never try to recoup losses by increasing your bet size. Risking more money will not change your luck or change the inherent odds of the game you are playing. If you are on a losing streak, bigger bets will only cause you to lose faster.

You need to recognize those specific instances when your best option is to quit playing. Although there are some situations that you will have to determine for yourself, the following list covers most of them:

> When you are losing.
> When you reached your loss limit.
> When you try to recoup by increasing your bet size.
> When you are not feeling well.
> When you are depressed.
> When you are tired.
> When you have sucked down too many free drinks.

If you are on a winning streak, however, grit your teeth and stick with it, even if you are unhappy, angry, or tired. Remember: Never quit while you are winning!

MONEY MANAGEMENT REMINDERS

- Never play with money that you can't afford to lose—your chances of losing are greater than your chances of winning.
- Never step up to a machine without first having designated specific funds for your gambling session.
- Never change your pre-established bankroll rules and dig for more money if you lose your allocated stake for the session or for the day. Instead, quit playing.
- Never deviate from smart playing strategy. And this book will tell you what that is.
- Never try to chase your losses.
- When you are winning, always set a loss limit.

DEALING WITH THE IRS

The relationship between gambling and the IRS is a complex subject that even confounds lawyers and accountants specializing in taxes. In this section, I am not giving you any specific tax or legal advice, but only making you aware of certain IRS requirements. It is valuable to know about some of these things before encountering them in a real situation.

If you engage in casino transactions of more than $10,000, you should consult an accountant familiar with gaming laws. Casinos must report all cash transactions in excess of $10,000 to the IRS. They must also report an aggregate of cash transactions that occur within a twenty-four-hour period and total more than $10,000. If you place a large bet at a sports book, cash-in chips, or even cash a check larger than $10,000, it must be reported. This is just a reporting requirement (presumably to control money laundering) and doesn't mean you have to pay taxes on the transaction. The state of Nevada also has a similar reporting requirement.

The IRS rule that is most important to gamblers is the requirement for the casino to report any lump sum win of $1200 or more by submitting a W-2G form. This, of course, refers mainly to slot machine jackpots, bingo prizes, and the like. Most table players don't have to worry about this requirement. For some odd reason that nobody can explain, the reporting requirement for keno is $1500 or more.

DID YOU KNOW...?

A single big win is not the only trigger for a W-2G form. If you won several small awards so that the credit total on your machine accumulated to $1200 or more when you cashed in, most casinos will submit a W-2G form. Avoid this by cashing out long before the credit total reaches that point.

If you won a lump sum during a tournament, however, the IRS reporting requirement drops to $600. For this kind of a win, the casino has to submit a 1099-MISC form.

Gambling winnings are considered ordinary income by the IRS and must be reported under "Other Income" on your 1040 tax return. If you are unfortunate enough to have a casino report your winnings, be sure you attach a copy of the W-2G or 1099-MISC to your return, or you will eventually get a letter from the IRS asking where it is.

If you are saddled with reported wins, you can reduce the tax burden (up to the amount of your winnings) if you can prove that you had offsetting gambling losses in the same year. Such losses cannot be subtracted from itemized winnings, but must be listed separately on Schedule A under "Miscellaneous Deductions." However, if your itemized deductions don't exceed the standard deduction, your gambling losses will not be useful as an offset. Also, keep in mind that you cannot reduce your overall tax by taking a net gambling loss—you can only offset winnings.

How do you prove that you had gambling losses? By keeping a detailed dairy of all your gambling activities. How detailed? The IRS recommendation is that you record the date, the time, the amount of your wins and losses, and the type of game. You should also record the name and location of the casino, and the names of any people (witnesses) with you at the time. Supporting documentation such as airline ticket receipts and hotel bills will help to convince an IRS auditor that you were actually there. However, unless you are a professional in the business of gambling and your trip was primarily for business purposes, do not try to deduct expenses such as transportation, hotel rooms, or restaurants.

Once you get used to the idea, you will see that keeping a diary is not as daunting as it first appears. How you actually deal with it, that is, what you put in and what you leave out, is entirely your decision. Just keep in mind that if the entire diary does not appear to be reasonable, an auditor may judge that it is inaccurate and disallow it.

But, you don't bother to keep a record because, like most people, you're there for just a few days and don't expect to hit a big jackpot.

You are smart enough, however, to join the slot club hoping that you will get a comp or two. It doesn't surprise you that after three days of playing the slots, you are down $1500. The fourth day you hit a $2000 jackpot, and after deducting the IRS withholding, the casino pays you less than $1500.

"What a bummer!" you complain. "I lose money and have to pay taxes, anyway!" A floor manager hears your griping and advises you to go to the slot club counter and get a record of your slot play. Sure enough, the record shows proof of your losses over the previous three days so that you can offset most of the jackpot winnings. Moral: Be sure to join the slot club—besides the normal club benefits, it can save you a bundle on taxes.

SLOT MACHINES
AND PAYBACKS

The purpose of this chapter is to give you information on the characteristics of your favorite slot machine and give you some guidance in your choice of which game to play. The machines on the following pages are currently found in casinos throughout the United States, and the information is the best available at the time this book was published. The games are listed in alphabetic order.

Although many games show several coinage denominations, a given casino may offer à particular game in only one or two denominations. The payback range shown for each game covers all the choices offered to the casino by the manufacturer. The exact payback is selected by the casino at the time the game is installed, and there is no way for a player to ascertain that specific number. The average hit frequency applies only when all the available paylines are activated. In some slot machines, the amount of the maximum bet is set by the casino. Progressive resets are subject to local gaming regulations, and can vary somewhat from jurisdiction to jurisdiction.

The large number of slot machines listed in this chapter represent only a portion of the wide variety of games that are on the casino floors. Keep in mind that the lifespan of a game is directly influenced by its popularity. Games that generate substandard income are soon replaced by the major casinos with new versions that the manufacturers are only too happy to provide. If you can no longer find a favorite game, try some of the smaller casinos because they can't afford to replace their machines as often.

ADDAMS FAMILY

Manufacturer:	International Game Technology
Game Format:	Bonus video, progressive
Number of Reels:	5
Number of Paylines:	1-9
Denomination:	Nickel
Maximum Bet:	45 credits
Top Payout:	Progressive
Progressive Reset:	$100,000 in Nevada
Average Hit Frequency:	44% (all lines active)
Long-term Payback Range:	89% to 90%

This spooky-themed game comes in a variety of configurations, all featuring an eerie aspect of the well-known Addams family. Each configuration has creative bonus games to add to the fun. The maximum wager to qualify for the MegaJackpot progressive is $2.25 (45 nickels), and the winner is paid in a lump sum. The reset is $100,000 in Nevada, but may vary in other jurisdictions.

ALL THAT GLITTERS

Manufacturer:	WMS Gaming
Game Format:	Bonus video
Number of Reels:	5
Number of Paylines:	1-20
Denominations:	All denominations
Maximum Bet:	20 to 400 credits
Top Payout:	25,000 credits
Average Hit Frequency:	37% to 39% (all lines active)
Long-term Payback Range:	84% to 95%

Instead of simulated spinning reels, jewel symbols fall down from the top of the screen. WMS calls this novel style of displaying the symbols Cascading Reels. Then, when any of the symbols form winning combinations, those symbols disappear and more jewels cascade down to fill the blank spaces. This continues until there are no winning combinations displayed. Each time a winning combination occurs, the appropriate number of credits is accumulated. Three bonus coin symbols on an active payline trigger a Jewelry Shop Bonus screen for extra credits.

CHAPTER 20 - SLOT MACHINES AND PAYBACKS

AMAZING WINS

Manufacturer:	Bally Technologies
Game Format:	Bonus video
Number of Reels:	5
Number of Paylines:	1-15
Denomination:	Penny
Maximum Bet:	750 credits
Top Payout:	Line bet times 10,000 credits
Average Hit Frequency:	28% (all lines active)
Long-term Payback Range:	88% to 96%

This game has a comfortable feel with all the classic slot machine symbols. It even has the pay table posted above the reels. Besides the expected wild multipliers, there are scatter symbols that trigger free spins. If you bet the maximum 50 credits per line, the top jackpot is $5,000.

ANCIENT FLAME

Manufacturer:	Konami Gaming
Game Format:	Bonus video
Number of Reels:	5
Number of Paylines:	None
Denominations:	Penny or two cents
Maximum Bet:	250 credits
Top Payout:	150,000 credits
Mystery Jackpot Thresholds:	$10 and $150
Average Hit Frequency:	45% (all reels active)
Long-term Payback Range:	87% to 89%

Each reel in this unusual game is a row of intermeshing hexagons. A winning combination occurs when at least three symbols connect on any of the six sides. The game is not a true progressive because the top jackpot is much larger than the two-level mystery progressives, which are won on a random basis after they reach their thresholds. There is also a scatter bonus that awards between 12 and 100 free spins.

ANDY CAPP

Manufacturer:	Bally Technologies
Game Format:	Bonus video
Number of Reels:	5
Number of Paylines:	1-9
Denominations:	Nickel or quarter
Maximum Bet:	45 credits
Top Payout:	25,000 credits
Average Hit Frequency:	47% (all lines active)
Long-term Payback Range:	86% to 94%

Based on working class Englishman Andy Capp and his long-suffering wife, Flo, this standard 9-line video game has two second-screen bonus events. When three dartboard symbols appear on reels one, three, and five, they are nudged to the center payline, transforming the center row of symbols to an animated scene that results in bonus awards and random free spins. The other event is triggered by three or more fence symbols and can pay up to 200 times the bet.

ANIMAL HOUSE

Manufacturer:	International Game Technology
Game Format:	Bonus video, progressive
Number of Reels:	5
Number of Paylines:	1-15
Denomination (stand-alone):	Multidenominational
Denomination (multisite):	Two cents
Maximum Bet:	150 credits
Top Payout:	Progressive
Progressive Reset:	$250,000
Average Hit Frequency:	50% (all lines active)
Long-term Payback Range:	88% to 90%

The two-cents version is a MegaJackpots progressive game; the multidenominational is a stand-alone progressive. The sounds and images are from the 1978 comedy film on which this game is based. The mechanical top box represents the Delta House fraternity and each of the six windows has a spinning reel, which is in addition to the scatter pay and video bonus awards. Lining up five Animal House symbols on the first payline, with a maximum bet, wins the progressive which is awarded as a lump sum.

ANYTHING BUT SIX!

Manufacturer:	International Game Technology
Game Format:	Bonus reel spinner
Number of Reels:	3
Number of Paylines:	5
Denomination:	Quarter or dollar
Maximum Bet:	5 coins
Top Payout:	5,500 coins
Average Hit Frequency:	30% (all lines active)
Long-term Payback Range:	85% to 98%

When three bar symbols land on a payline, a jackpot is paid and the bonus top box lights up, along with the bonus ladder that starts at 15 coins and climbs to 1,100 coins at the top. If the player chooses to risk the jackpot, a large die in the top box rolls to advance lights up the ladder, so long as a six is not rolled. The bonus continues until the player decides to collect, or rolls a six, which wipes out the wins. If the player reaches the top, he wins 1,100 credits times the total bet.

ASIAN PRINCESS

Manufacturer:	Aristocrat Technologies
Game Format:	Bonus video
Number of Reels:	5
Number of Paylines:	Scatter pay
Denominations:	Penny, two cents, or nickel
Maximum Bet:	500 or 1,000 credits
Top Payout (500-credit version):	300,000 credits
Top Payout (1,000-credit version):	600,000 credits
Average Hit Frequency:	70% (all reels active)
Long-term Payback Range:	88% to 97%

In this game the player pays to activate reels instead of paylines, however, there are no paylines. All wins are based on scatter symbols. When a player makes an extra ante bet, the screen is transformed so that each reel has five symbols instead of the usual three. Then, with all reels activated, every spin has 3,125 possible winning combinations. Triggering the secondary screen starts a special free-spin bonus round with up to 25 free spins and up to a 5X jackpot multiplier.

AUSTIN POWERS IN GOLDMEMBER

Manufacturer:	International Game Technology
Game Format:	Bonus video, progressive
Number of Reels:	5
Number of Paylines:	1-15
Denomination:	Nickel
Maximum Bet:	75 credits
Top Payout:	Progressive
Progressive Reset:	$100,000
Average Hit Frequency:	50% (all lines active)
Long-term Payback Range:	88% to 90%

The voice-over in this MegaJackpots game is provided by Mike Meyers. The progressive jackpot is paid when five logo symbols are lined up on the 15th payline and the maximum bet was wagered. The jackpot is paid as a lump sum. There are two bonus events, one of which displays clips from the movie and reveals a credit multiplier of from 3 to 24 times the total wager. The other one shows silhouettes of several She-Spy characters and awards free spins.

AVALANCHE OF CASH

Manufacturer:	Atronic Americas
Game Format:	Bonus video
Number of Reels:	5
Number of Paylines:	1-9, 1-15, or 1-21
Denominations:	Penny, two cents, nickel, or quarter
Maximum Bet:	27 to 210 credits
Top Payout (9- and 15-line versions):	30,000 credits
Top Payout (21-line version):	100,000 credits
Average Hit Frequency (9-line):	27% (all lines active)
Average Hit Frequency (15-line):	35% (all lines active)
Average Hit Frequency (21-line):	39% (all lines active)
Long-term Payback Range:	86% to 94%

Instead of an avalanche of snow, we have an avalanche of cash in this arctic-themed game. Three or more flag symbols on reels one, three, and five, trigger the Flag Bonus in which the symbols transform into credit amounts. Three or more Avalanche symbols anywhere on the middle three reels starts the Avalanche of Free Games bonus, where the player is given the choice of 20 free spins with no multiplier, 10 free spins at 2X, seven free spins at 3X, or five free spins at 4X. With a maximum wager, five Yeti symbols on a payline wins the top jackpot.

AZTEC TEMPLE

Manufacturer:	International Game Technology
Game Format:	Bonus video
Number of Reels:	5
Number of Paylines:	Scatter pay
Denominations:	Penny
Maximum Bet:	1,250 credits
Top Payout:	125,000 credits
Average Hit Frequency:	41% (all reels active)
Long-term Payback Range:	85% to 98%

Instead of activating paylines, in this game the player pays to activate the reels, at five credits per reel. All wins are based on scatter symbols, and with all reels activated, every spin has 243 possible winning combinations. Triggering the bonus event causes gold medallion symbols to appear on the screen. The player is prompted to select one of them which results in a random number of free spins, along with a win multiplier of up to 5X.

BAMBOO FOREST

Manufacturer:	Atronic Americas
Game Format:	Bonus video
Number of Reels:	5
Number of Paylines:	1-9 or 1-21
Denominations:	Penny, two cents, or nickel
Maximum Bet:	27, 90, 210, or 525 credits
Top Payout (9-line, 27-credit version):	30,000 credits
Top Payout (9-line, 90-credit version):	100,000 credits
Top Payout (21-line, 210-credit version):	200,000 credits
Top Payout (21-line, 525-credit version):	500,000 credits
Average Hit Frequency (9-line):	32% (all lines active)
Average Hit Frequency (21-line):	49% (all lines active)
Long-term Payback Range:	86% to 96%

The theme is a magical oriental bamboo forest with panda bears. The game has numerous bonus features, and the player can choose to have all winning combinations left-to-right or both left-to-right and right-to-left. There is also a Spin-As-Long-As-You-Win feature where the free spins continue as long as you get at least one winning combination. Some bonuses start with three or more payline symbols and others start with scatter symbols.

BANKROLL

Manufacturer:	AC Coin and Slot
Game Format:	Bonus reel spinner, option buy
Number of Reels:	3
Number of Paylines:	1 or 5
Denominations:	Quarter, half, or dollar
Maximum Bet (1-line version):	3 coins
Maximum Bet (5-line version):	5 coins
Top Payout:	Various
Average Hit Frequency:	12% to 14% (all lines active)
Long Term Payback Range:	87% to 93%

This slot comes in three different base games, all of which are popular IGT reel spinners. An extra Bankroll symbol on the third reel triggers the top-box bonus event. The sheet of bills next to Uncle Sam starts scrolling and the arrows at the bottom begin to flash in sequence. The player is awarded the amount on the bill next to the lit arrow. If it is a multiplier, the scrolling begins again until the lit arrow points to a bonus amount, that is then multiplied accordingly.

BETTY BOOP SERIES

Betty Boop's All American Girl
Betty Boop's Blazing 7s
Betty Boop's Born to Boop
Betty Boop's Double Jackpot
Betty Boop's Roaring 20s
Betty Boop's Swing Time Betty

Manufacturer:	Bally Technologies
Game Format:	Reel spinner, progressive or option-buy
Number of Reels:	3
Number of Paylines:	1
Denominations:	Nickel, quarter, or dollar
Maximum Bet (nickel):	5 coins
Maximum Bet (quarter):	3 coins
Maximum Bet (dollar):	2 coins
Top Payout (nickel):	2 million coins
Top Payout (quarter):	400,000 coins
Top Payout (dollar):	100,000 coins
Top Payout (multisite):	Progressive
Progressive Reset:	$100,000
Average Hit Frequency:	36% to 38%
Long-term Payback Range (nickel):	84%
Long-term Payback Range (quarter):	86%
Long-term Payback Range (dollar):	88%

Betty Boop is one of Bally's most popular icons, and many of their games are based on this character. Although there are some minor differences, all the above games are essentially similar. These are all option-buy games, so even if you play the non-progressive version, you must bet the maximum amount to win the jackpots. The progressive version is linked to Bally's Blondie and Popeye slots.

THE BEVERLY HILLBILLIES – CASH FOR CRUDE

Manufacturer:	International Game Technology
Game Format:	Bonus video, progressive
Number of Reels:	5
Number of Paylines:	1-25
Denomination:	Penny
Maximum Bet:	150 credits
Top Payout:	Progressive
Progressive Reset:	$1 million
Average Hit Frequency:	50% (all lines active)
Long-term Payback:	85% to 88%

Animated reel symbols reflect characters from the popular 1960s sitcom. This MegaJackpots progressive features an oil derrick in the top box bonus feature. Cash for Crude symbols in any position on the three middle reels starts the bonus, which also requires the player to bet at least one credit per payline plus a five-credit ante. To qualify for the progressive, however, takes the maximum wager of 150 credits.

BEWITCHED SPIN

Manufacturer:	AC Coin and Slot
Game Format:	Bonus reel spinner
Number of Reels:	3
Number of Paylines:	1-5 or 1-9
Denominations:	All denominations
Maximum Bet (5-line version):	75 credits
Maximum Bet (9-line version):	135 credits
Top Payout:	100,000 credits
Average Hit Frequency:	50% (all lines active)
Long Term Payback Range:	85% to 95%

The game is based on the IGT Triple Stars three-reel slot with the same set of symbols. When three Bewitched symbols land on a payline, lights begin to flash. They flash around the circular game board until they stop to award a number of bonus balls or a multiplier. The Slotto sphere then circulates the balls on air until they drop into a chute. After counting up all the credit awards and multipliers, the result is multiplied by the line wager.

BIG BEN

Manufacturer:	Aristocrat Technologies
Game Format:	Bonus video, progressive
Number of Reels:	5
Number of Paylines:	1-15, 1-20, or 1-25
Denominations:	Penny or nickel
Maximum Bet:	150 or 200 credits
Top Payout (non-progressive):	Line bet times 60,000 credits
Progressive Reset:	Set by casino
Average Hit Frequency:	45% (all lines active)
Long-term Payback Range:	88% to 97%

The progressive jackpot in this London-themed game can be won by a payline combination or in either of the two bonus features. One bonus is a free-spin round with multiplied jackpots. The other bonus is a second screen that displays the Big Ben clock. Each chime of the clock raises the credit award, and if it chimes twelve times, wins the progressive. The game can also be set up as a non-progressive with a jackpot of 60,000 credits times the line bet.

BIG RED 2

Manufacturer:	Aristocrat Technologies
Game Format:	Bonus video, progressive
Number of Reels:	5
Number of Paylines:	1-5
Denominations:	Nickel or dollar
Maximum Bet:	25 credits (Nevada), 50 credits (elsewhere)
Top Payout:	Progressive
Progressive Reset (major):	$1,000 (typical)
Progressive Reset (minor):	$250 (typical)
Average Hit Frequency:	25% (all lines active)
Long-term Payback Range:	91% to 95%

This is a double stand-alone progressive that has an Australian theme with a cartoon kangaroo character named Big Red. The kangaroo symbol is wild and when one or more appear in a winning combination, the player is awarded five free spins for each active payline. The free spin round is when the progressives can be won, and this occurs when Dingo symbols land on the first and fifth reel. The reset levels can be set by the casino up to $3,000.

BINGO NIGHTS SLOTTO

Manufacturer:	AC Coin and Slot
Game Format:	Bonus reel spinner
Number of Reels:	5
Number of Paylines:	1-9
Denominations:	Penny, two cents, or nickel
Maximum Bet:	45 or 180 coins
Top Payout (45-coin version):	25,000 coins
Top Payout (180-coin version):	100,000 coins
Average Hit Frequency:	50% (all lines active)
Long-term Payback Range:	87% to 92%

This is a reel spinning format that behaves more like a video slot, and features a mechanical top-box bonus. The base game is the IGT Double Diamond game in the five-reel version, using all the standard IGT reel symbols. When the top box bingo bonus event is triggered, the bingo tumbler begins to rotate and a bingo card is displayed. Five wild symbols on a payline wins the top jackpot.

BLASTIN' BARRELS

Manufacturer:	Atronic Americas
Game Format:	Bonus video, progressive
Number of Reels:	5
Number of Paylines:	1-9 or 1-21
Denominations:	Penny or nickel
Maximum Bet (9-line version):	27, 45, or 90 credits
Maximum Bet (21-line version):	63 or 210 credits
Top Payout:	Progressive
Progressive Reset:	$50,000
Average Hit Frequency:	50% (all lines active)
Long-term Payback Range:	86% to 94%

This game, with a whimsical fairy tale theme, is a conventional video slot with low volatility and plenty of bonus features. Lining up five Gold Seeker symbols at maximum bet wins the progressive. In addition to a bonus round, the game includes substitute symbols, scatter symbols, and very elaborate free-spin awards that can last for up to 300 free spins.

BLAZING 7s (three-reel)

Manufacturer:	Bally Technologies
Game Format:	Reel spinner, option-buy
Number of Reels:	3
Number of Paylines:	1
Denominations:	Quarter, half, or dollar
Maximum Bet:	2 or 3 coins
Top Payout:	1,000, 1,500, or 2,000 coins
Average Hit Frequency:	14%
Long-term Payback Range:	84% to 98%

This is the most popular of the Bally reel spinners. It's a classic three-reel option-buy game that comes in a two- or three-coin version. Because it's an option-buy, it should only be played with a maximum wager.

BLAZING 7s (five-reel)

Manufacturer:	Bally Technologies
Game Format:	Reel spinner, option-buy
Number of Reels:	5
Number of Paylines:	1
Denomination:	Quarter
Maximum Bet:	5 coins
Top Payout:	20,000 coins
Average Hit Frequency:	21%
Long-term Payback Range:	81% to 97%

A five-reel version of Bally's classic reel spinner. Besides the five reels, it has one idiosyncrasy (for an option-buy machine): you don't have to make the maximum wager of five coins to qualify for all the jackpots. Four coins is enough.

BLAZING 7s (video)

Manufacturer:	Bally Technologies
Game Format:	Bonus video
Number of Reels:	5
Number of Paylines:	1-9
Denomination:	Nickel
Maximum Bet:	27 credits
Top Payout:	$1,000
Average Hit Frequency:	59% (all lines active)
Long-term Payback Range:	87% to 95%

With the payout table posted above the reels, this video version of Bally's classic slot game emulates a reel spinner. Line up five Blazing 7s on a payline and win the top jackpot, assuming you bet the maximum amount. There are no bonus events, but with one of the highest hit frequencies of all slots, it doesn't need one. To get that hit frequency, you only need to wager one nickel per line—a 45¢ bet.

BLUES BROTHERS

Manufacturer:	Bally Technologies
Game Format:	Bonus video
Number of Reels:	5
Number of Paylines:	1-20
Denomination:	Penny
Maximum Bet:	1,000 credits
Top Payout:	Line bet times 10,000 credits
Average Hit Frequency:	28% (all lines active)
Long-term Payback Range:	88% to 96%

All the major Blues Brothers images appear as symbols on the reels. When briefcase symbols land on the first, third, and fifth reels, a bonus equal to three times the total wager is paid. Three or more scattered free games symbols results in a random number of free spins with tripled jackpots.

BOMBAY

Manufacturer:	International Game Technology
Game Format:	Bonus video
Number of Reels:	5
Number of Paylines:	1-100
Denomination:	Penny
Maximum Bet:	2,000 credits
Top Payout:	200,000 credits
Average Hit Frequency:	24% (all lines active)
Long-term Payback Range:	92% to 98%

This game features 100 paylines on a five-by-five screen configuration with oversized symbols. Three or more bonus symbols on an active payline starts a free-spin bonus event. The player is given at least five free spins, and additional spins can be awarded during the free-spin round up to a maximum of 325. Lining up five Bombay symbols on a payline wins the top jackpot of $2,000.

BONUS HOT DOGS DELUXE

All Stars
Diamond Dogs
Super Bonus

Manufacturer:	AC Coin and Slot
Game Format:	Reel spinner, option-buy
Number of Reels:	3
Number of Paylines:	1 or 5
Denominations:	All denominations from quarter to $50
Maximum Bet:	3 or 5 coins
Top Payout:	2,400, 6,000, or 7,500 coins
Average Hit Frequency (1-line):	14%
Average Hit Frequency (5-line):	40% (all lines active)
Payback Range (All Stars):	85% to 95%
Payback Range (Diamond Dogs):	89% to 93%
Payback Range (Super Bonus):	89% to 96%

This game comes in three versions that have a wide range of denominations. Diamond Dogs and Super Bonus are one-payline, three-coin games, while All Stars is a five-payline, five-coin version. Since these are option-buy (buy-a-pay) games, activating the bonus event requires a maximum wager to give the player any chance of winning the top award.

BONUS PARTY

Manufacturer:	AC Coin and Slot
Game Format:	Bonus reel spinner
Number of Reels:	5
Number of Paylines:	1-9
Denomination:	Penny
Maximum Bet:	45 or 180 coins
Top Payout (non-progressive):	$250 (45 coin), $1,000 (180 coin)
Progressive Reset:	$5,000
Average Hit Frequency:	50% (all lines active)
Long-term Payback Range:	86% to 92%

This is a reel spinning format that behaves more like a video slot, and features a top-box bonus event that depicts a disco party. There is one progressive and two non-progressive versions, and they are based on the IGT Double Diamond game. When the top box bonus is triggered, the player is prompted to push a flashing button that starts a vertical scroll showing a different party scene on each floor.

BONUS TIMES

Manufacturer:	Bally Technologies
Game Format:	Bonus video
Number of Reels:	5
Number of Paylines:	1-5 or 1-20
Denominations:	All denominations
Maximum Bet (5-line version):	75 credits
Maximum Bet (20-line version):	1,000 credits
Top Payout:	6,000 credits
Average Hit Frequency (5-line):	25% (all lines active)
Average Hit Frequency (20-line):	50% (all lines active)
Long-term Payback Range:	86% to 94%

The name of this game refers to the wild symbol multipliers, which can be 2X, 3X, and/or 5X. Besides being wild, the symbols multiply the jackpots in winning combinations. If more than one of the wild symbols fall on a payline, they multiply together, which can result in a large credit win.

BOXCAR BONUS

Manufacturer:	Bally Technologies
Game Format:	Bonus video
Number of Reels:	5
Number of Paylines:	1-25
Denomination:	Penny
Maximum Bet:	1,250 credits
Top Payout:	Line bet times 5,000 credits ($2,500)
Average Hit Frequency:	57% (all lines active)
Long-term Payback Range:	88% to 96%

In this railroad-themed game, the boxcar bonus is triggered by boxcar symbols landing in any position on all five reels. The second screen depicts a cartoon train that eventually pulls into a train station, where the player is prompted by the cartoon conductor to select one of three boxcars. The resulting bonus award ranges from 5 to 180 times the total wager. This game can be configured for other denominations and can also be configured for a progressive award.

BRAZILIAN BEAUTY

Manufacturer:	WMS Gaming
Game Format:	Bonus video
Number of Reels:	5
Number of Paylines:	1-5, 1-9, 1-20, 1-25, or 1-30
Denominations:	All denominations from penny to dollar
Maximum Bet (5-line version):	150 credits
Maximum Bet (9-line version):	270 credits
Maximum Bet (20-line version):	600 credits
Maximum Bet (25-line version):	750 credits
Maximum Bet (30-line version):	900 credits
Top Payout:	270,000 credits
Average Hit Frequency:	16% to 47% (all lines active)
Long-term Payback Range:	87% to 96%

This Latin-themed game comes in quite a few varieties and denominations. When three or more Sun God scatter symbols appear anywhere on the reels, a free-spin bonus of 10 to 20 spins will begin. During the free-spin period, the free-spin round can be retriggered and Beauty symbols will be collected for credit awards. If 20 Beauty symbols are accumulated, the bonus award is 300 times the wager.

CALIFORNIA DREAMIN' (line game)

Manufacturer:	Bally Technologies
Game Format:	Reel spinner, line game
Number of Reels:	3
Number of Paylines:	3
Denominations:	Nickel, quarter, or dollar
Maximum Bet:	3 coins
Top Payout:	2,500 coins
Average Hit Frequency:	12% (all lines active)
Long-term Payback Range:	86% to 97%

A classic three-reel line game that comes in a three-line, three-coin version in three different denominations. Like most of the old reel spinners, it has a low hit frequency.

CALIFORNIA DREAMIN' (multiplier)

Manufacturer:	Bally Technologies
Game Format:	Reel spinner, multiplier
Number of Reels:	3
Number of Paylines:	1
Denominations:	Nickel, quarter, or dollar
Maximum Bet:	2 or 3 coins
Top Payout (2-coin version):	1,600 coins
Top Payout (3-coin version):	2,500 coins
Average Hit Frequency:	13% to 15%
Long-term Payback Range:	84% to 97%

A classic 3-reel multiplier that comes in a two- or three-coin version. The two coin version is a true multiplier, while three-coin version is a near-true multiplier. This is a good game for a novice player.

CAPTAIN JACKPOT

Manufacturer:	Bally Technologies
Game Format:	Bonus video
Number of Reels:	5
Number of Paylines:	1-15
Denominations:	Nickel or quarter
Maximum Bet:	15 to 450 credits, casino adjustable
Top Payout:	Line bet times 10,000 credits
Average Hit Frequency:	48% (all lines active)
Long-term Payback Range:	90% to 94%

The slot operator can set the maximum bet on this machine from one credit per payline to 30 credits per payline. The only bonus feature is a free-spin round, which can only be activated with a maximum credit bet. This bonus round occurs an average of every 124 spins, but when it happens, it can result in a big payback.

CARNIVAL OF MYSTERY

Manufacturer:	International Game Technology
Game Format:	Bonus video
Number of Reels:	5
Number of Paylines:	Scatter pay
Denominations:	Penny
Maximum Bet:	1,250 credits
Top Payout:	250,000 credits
Average Hit Frequency:	70% (all reels active)
Long-term Payback Range:	85% to 98%

In this game, with a carnival theme, the player pays to activate the reels instead of paylines, and all wins are based on scatter symbols. The maximum wager brings to bear every winning combination, for a total of 243 possibilities. The main bonus sequence contains three sub-bonus events in which the player collects credits or a ticket to one of the other sub-bonuses.

CHURCH LADY

Manufacturer:	Bally Technologies
Game Format:	Bonus video
Number of Reels:	5
Number of Paylines:	1-9
Denominations:	Nickel or quarter
Maximum Bet:	18, 27, or 45 coins
Top Payout:	$10,000
Average Hit Frequency:	41% (all lines active)
Long-term Payback Range:	88% to 92%

Based on Dana Carvey's SNL character, Carvey did the voice-overs for the audio effects. This game has two second-screen bonuses. Three canned ham symbols on the middle three reels start the Canned Ham bonus round, in which the player is prompted to pick one of three dancing hams to win an award. Three adjacent Church Chat symbols on a payline activate the main bonus feature that is a three-tiered sequence paying 16 to 850 times the line bet.

CLEOPATRA

Manufacturer:	International Game Technology
Game Format:	Bonus video
Number of Reels:	5
Number of Paylines:	1-9 or 1-20
Denominations:	All denominations
Maximum Bet (9-line version):	45 or 180 credits
Maximum Bet (20-line version):	100 or 400 credits
Top Payout (9-line):	50,000 credits
Top Payout (20-line):	200,000 credits
Average Hit Frequency:	36% (all lines active)
Long-term Payback Range:	85% to 98%

As you would guess, the theme is ancient Egypt. The main bonus gives you a scatter payout and 15 free spins, during which time you can win up to 300 times the credits wagered. During the free-spin period, the bonus can be doubled and another free-spin bonus can be triggered.

CLUB MOULIN

Manufacturer:	Konami Gaming
Game Format:	Bonus video
Number of Reels:	5
Number of Paylines:	1-10, 1-20, 1-25, or 1-30
Denominations:	Penny, two cents, or nickel
Maximum Bet:	30 to 3,000 credits
Top Payout:	Line bet times 2,000 credits
Mystery Jackpot Thresholds:	$100 (Mini) and $1,000 (Major)
Average Hit Frequency:	75% (all lines active)
Long-term Payback Range:	85% to 96%

The historic Club Moulin in Paris is the theme, with images of champagne and can-can dancers. Three or more scatter symbols start the bonus round with an award of 13 to 25 free spins and all jackpots doubled. More free spins can be won during the free-spin round. The mystery progressive feature is not dependent on any symbol combination, but is awarded randomly after it reaches the threshold. The Mini progressive has a range of up to $1,000, and the Major can reach $2,000.

COOL CAT CASH

Manufacturer:	WMS Gaming
Game Format:	Bonus video
Number of Reels:	5
Number of Paylines:	1-15, 1-20, or 1-25
Denominations:	All denominations
Maximum Bet (15-line version):	15-300 credits
Maximum Bet (20-line version):	20-400 credits
Maximum Bet (25-line version):	25-500 credits
Top Payout:	50,000 credits (all versions)
Average Hit Frequency (15-line):	33% to 35% (all lines active)
Average Hit Frequency (20-line):	40% to 41% (all lines active)
Average Hit Frequency (25-line):	47% to 49% (all lines active)
Long-term Payback Range:	84% to 95%

This game is available to the casino in a large number of configurations involving the number of paylines, maximum bet, and denomination. Expect to find mainly penny, two cents, and nickel denominations. There are two main bonus features. The Super Scatter bonus can result in up to 15 free spins with all wins paid as scatters. The other bonus is a second screen event with a grid of 20 safes, and the player gets to select five of them.

COYOTE MOON

Manufacturer:	International Game Technology
Game Format:	Bonus video
Number of Reels:	5
Number of Paylines:	1-40
Denomination:	Penny
Maximum Bet:	400 credits
Top Payout:	50,000 credits
Average Hit Frequency:	17% (all lines active)
Long-term Payback Range:	88% to 98%

When bonus symbols appear on the three middle reels in any position, the free-spin feature is triggered and the player is awarded five free spins. If the bonus symbols land again during a free spin, another five is awarded. This can go on for a maximum of 255 free spins. Wild symbols also add to the accumulation of credits.

CRIMSON FIRE

Manufacturer:	Atronic Americas
Game Format:	Bonus video
Number of Reels:	5
Number of Paylines:	1-50
Denominations:	All denominations
Maximum Bet:	500 or 1,000 credits
Top Payout (500-credit version):	Line bet times 5,000 credits
Top Payout (1,000-credit version):	Line bet times 10,000 credits
Average Hit Frequency:	32% (all lines active)
Long-term Payback Range:	86% to 96%

The moon symbol is wild for all but the chest symbol, which is a scatter symbol. When three chest symbols land anywhere on reels 1, 2, and 3, the player is awarded 10 free spins. During those free spins, additional wild moon symbols are added which increases the chances of retriggering the free spins feature during a free spin.

THE DATING GAME

Manufacturer:	International Game Technology
Game Format:	Bonus video, progressive
Number of Reels:	5
Number of Paylines:	1-15
Denominations:	Nickel or quarter
Maximum Bet (nickel):	75 credits
Maximum Bet (quarter):	20 credits
Top Payout:	Progressive
Progressive Reset:	$100,000
Average Hit Frequency:	50% (all lines active)
Long-term Payback:	89%

Although this is a MegaJackpots multisite progressive game, there are two bonus events, which can result in as many as 200 free spins. The voice-over is done by Jim Lange, who hosted the Dating Game TV show for a long time. The progressive jackpot is won by lining up five Dating Game symbols on the first payline, and is only paid out for maximum bets. It is awarded as a lump sum.

DEAL OR NO DEAL (bonus video)

Manufacturer:	Atronic Americas
Game Format:	Bonus video
Number of Reels:	5
Number of Paylines:	1-5, 1-9, 1-15, or 1-21
Denominations:	Penny, nickel, quarter, dollar, $5, or $10
Maximum Bet:	50, 90, 150, or 210
Top Payout (5-line version):	10,000 or 50,000 credits
Top Payout (9-line version):	30,000 to 1 million credits
Top Payout (15-line version):	30,000 credits
Top Payout (21-line version):	10,000 to 500,000 credits
Average Hit Frequency (5-line):	30% (all lines active)
Average Hit Frequency (9-line):	35% (all lines active)
Average Hit Frequency (15-line):	40% (all lines active)
Average Hit Frequency (21-line):	50% (all lines active)
Long-term Payback Range:	86% to 96%

Another game show theme. This game has two main bonus events as well as several secondary events. Four versions are available with different numbers of paylines. Note that although the 21-line version has almost double the 5-line hit frequency, it costs more than four times as much to play all the paylines. One of the two main bonus events resolves into one of three possible secondary events resulting in a string of bonus awards and bonus multipliers.

DEAL OR NO DEAL (progressive)

Manufacturer:	Atronic Americas
Game Format:	Bonus video, progressive
Number of Reels:	5
Number of Paylines:	1-9 or 1-21
Denominations:	Penny, two cents, or nickel
Maximum Bet:	45, 90, 105, or 210 credits
Top Payout:	Progressive
Progressive Reset (penny version):	$500
Progressive Reset (nickel version):	$2,500
Average Hit Frequency (9-line version):	40% (all lines active)
Average Hit Frequency (21-line version):	49% (all lines active)
Long-term Payback Range:	88% to 92%

Based on the popular Howie Mandell show, this game has three bonus events as well as a progressive jackpot. There are two theme variations and two payline variations for each theme. The progressive jackpot can be won five different ways in addition to a mystery feature that awards the jackpot randomly.

DEEP BLUE DOLLAR$

Manufacturer:	Atronic Americas
Game Format:	Bonus video or progressive
Number of Reels:	5
Number of Paylines:	1-5, 1-9, or 1-20
Denominations:	Penny, two cents, nickel, or quarter
Maximum Bet (5-line version):	25 credits
Maximum Bet (9-line version):	45 credits
Maximum Bet (20-line version):	100 credits
Top Payout:	Progressive or 50,000 credits for non-progressive
Progressive Reset:	Set by casino
Average Hit Frequency (5-line):	29% (all lines active)
Average Hit Frequency (9-line):	37% (all lines active)
Average Hit Frequency (20-line):	44% (all lines active)
Long-term Payback Range:	88% to 98%

Three payline configurations are available with the main bonus being a free spin feature. Three or more dollar symbols on a payline starts a bonus that awards the player with 15 free spins, with all jackpots doubled. A black pearl on the fifth reel during a free spin increases the multiplier to 3X. This game is also available as a progressive with the jackpot amount set by the casino, and that is won with five mask symbols.

DIAMOND EYES!

Manufacturer:	Aristocrat Technologies
Game Format:	Bonus video
Number of Reels:	5
Number of Paylines:	1-15 or 1-25
Denominations:	Penny, two cents, or nickel
Maximum Bet (15-line version):	75, 150, 300, or 600 credits
Maximum Bet (25-line version):	125, 250, 500, or 1,000 credits
Top Payout:	7,500, 15,000, 30,000, or 60,000 credits
Average Hit Frequency:	45% (all lines active)
Long-term Payback Range:	88% to 97%

All the winning combinations in this game pay right to left as well as the traditional left to right, starting at the outer reels. The game also has scatter-pay combinations. Although it has a high hit frequency, the only bonus in this game is a free spin round that gives the player ten free spins. This award can be repeated during the free-spin round.

DIAMOND FORTUNE

Manufacturer:	Konami Gaming
Game Format:	Bonus reel spinner
Number of Reels:	3
Number of Paylines:	Scatter
Denominations:	All denominations from penny to $1
Maximum Bet:	750 coins
Top Payout:	Bet times 81,020 coins
Average Hit Frequency:	30% (all reels active)
Long-term Payback Range:	86% to 98%

This unusual format is a three-reel game with no paylines; all wins are scatter-pay. The fourth reel is actually an LCD screen that serves as a bonus multiplier. There are 2X, 3X, and 5X multiplying wild symbols on the three main reels, and up to 10X multipliers on the fourth reel. Furthermore, all wins are multiplied by the amount of the bet.

DIAMOND LINE FRENZY

Manufacturer:	Bally Technologies
Game Format:	Reel spinner, option-buy
Number of Reels:	4
Number of Paylines:	2
Denominations:	Quarter, half, or dollar
Maximum Bet:	3 coins
Top Payout:	10,000 coins
Average Hit Frequency:	15% (all lines active)
Long-term Payback Range:	88% to 97%

Strictly speaking this is a four-reel game, although the fourth reel only shows bonus multipliers and a re-spin symbol. The two paylines consist of one across the center and a second in the shape of a diamond. Remember, this is an option-buy (buy-a-pay) game: the first coin activates the center payline, the second coin activates the diamond payline, and the third coin activates the bonus reel. You must play maximum coins.

DIAMONDS AND DEVILS

Manufacturer:	Bally Technologies
Game Format:	Bonus reel spinner, progressive
Number of Reels:	5
Number of Paylines:	1-25
Denominations:	All denominations from penny to dollar
Maximum Bet:	75 coins
Top Payout:	Progressive
Progressive Reset (penny):	$10, $100, and $1,000
Progressive Reset (other denoms):	Up to $100,000 for top jackpot
Average Hit Frequency:	50% (all lines active)
Long-term Payback Range:	86% to 96%

This reel spinner acts more like a bonus video slot. The video top box displays three progressive amounts that can be won with three, four, or five diamond symbols on an active payline with maximum coins. In addition, when the devil symbols appear in the correct positions on the reels, there is a free-spin bonus feature with a random multiplier.

DIAMONDS AND ROSES

Manufacturer:	Bally Technologies
Game Format:	Reel spinner, multiplier
Number of Reels:	3
Number of Paylines:	1
Denominations:	Nickel, dime, quarter, half, or dollar
Maximum Bet:	2 or 3 coins
Top Payout (2-coin version):	2,500 coins
Top Payout (3-coin version):	4,000 coins
Average Hit Frequency:	14%
Long-term Payback Range:	83% to 97%

One of the classic Bally reel spinners, this is a three-reel, one-payline multiplier that comes in two- and three-coin versions.

DIAMOND SOLITAIRE

Manufacturer:	Konami Gaming
Game Format:	Reel spinner, option-buy
Number of Reels:	3
Number of Paylines:	1
Denominations:	Nickel, quarter, dollar, $2, or $5
Maximum Bet:	3 coins
Top Payout:	15,000 coins
Average Hit Frequency:	16%
Long-term Payback Range:	85% to 98%

Although this seems like a four-reel game, the fourth reel only shows a bonus screen, which can be activated only with a maximum 3-coin bet. This is an option-buy (buy-a-pay) game, so you must play maximum coins to win the top jackpot or any of the bonuses. One of the bonuses is a free-spin event.

DIRTY HARRY: MAKE MY DAY

Manufacturer:	WMS Gaming
Game Format:	Bonus video or progressive
Number of Reels:	5
Number of Paylines:	1-20 or 1-30
Denominations:	Penny or nickel
Maximum Bet (20-line version):	200 credits
Maximum Bet (30-line version):	60 credits
Top Payout	
(non-progressive version):	10,000 credits
Reset (multisite progressive):	$500,000
Average Hit Frequency:	53% to 56% (all lines active)
Long-term Payback Range:	86% to 94%

This is another WMS game with sensory immersion technology. The surround sound and vibrating seat make you feel that you're actually in the patrol car, chasing the bad guys. It may seem like a realistic video game, but it's a very good slot game with a high hit frequency. With all paylines activated, three scattered Make My Day symbols starts a police chase through San Francisco. The player chooses a police car and a target for Harry to shoot at. If the shot misses, and the criminal shoots back, hitting Harry's car, the bonus round ends. If Harry's shot hits the criminal's car, it swerves into bonus awards and may crash into a Catch symbol, in which case, the criminal is caught and a new chase begins.

DOUBLE DIAMOND (reel)

Manufacturer:	International Game Technology
Game Format:	Reel spinner, multiplier
Number of Reels:	3
Number of Paylines:	1
Denominations:	All or multidenominational
Maximum Bet:	1, 2, or 3 coins
Top Payout:	800, 1,600, or 2,500 coins
Average Hit Frequency:	14%
Long-term Payback Range:	85% to 98%

An old favorite IGT three-reel multiplier with a single payline that comes in one-, two-, and three-coin versions. After twenty years, it still hasn't faded.

DOUBLE DIAMOND (video)

Manufacturer:	International Game Technology
Game Format:	Video, reel emulator
Number of Reels:	3
Number of Paylines:	1-5 or 1-9
Denominations:	.All or multidenominational
Maximum Bet (5-line version):	100 credits
Maximum Bet (9-line version):	180 credits
Top Payout:	100,000 credits
Average Hit Frequency:	59% (all lines active)
Long-term Payback Range:	85% to 98%

This is a five- and nine-line version of the spinning reel game with the addition of scatter symbol and nudge symbol bonuses, and a very high hit frequency.

DOUBLE DIAMOND DELUXE

Manufacturer:	International Game Technology
Game Format:	Reel spinner, multiplier
Number of Reels:	3
Number of Paylines:	1
Denominations:	All or multidenominational
Maximum Bet:	1, 2, or 3 coins
Top Payout (1-coin version):	1,000 coins
Top Payout (2-coin version):	1,600 coins
Top Payout (3-coin version):	2,500 coins
Average Hit Frequency:	14%
Long-term Payback Range:	85% to 98%

A classic three-reel multiplier with a single payline that comes in one-, two-, and three-coin versions.

DOUBLE RED, WHITE & BLUE

Manufacturer:	International Game Technology
Game Format:	Reel spinner, modified multiplier
Number of Reels:	3
Number of Paylines:	1
Denominations:	All or multidenominational
Maximum Bet:	1, 2, or 3 coins
Top Payout (1-coin version):	1,200 coins
Top Payout (2-coin version):	5,000 coins
Top Payout (3-coin version):	10,000 coins
Average Hit Frequency:	20%
Long-term Payback Range:	85% to 98%

A classic three-reel modified multiplier with a single payline that comes in one-, two-, and three-coin versions.

DOUBLE TRIPLE DIAMOND DELUXE WITH CHEESE

Manufacturer:	International Game Technology
Game Format:	Reel spinner, option-buy
Number of Reels:	3
Number of Paylines:	1
Denominations:	Quarter or dollar
Maximum Bet:	3 coins
Top Payout:	15,000 coins
Average Hit Frequency:	15%
Long-term Payback Range:	88% to 96%

IGT modified their Double Triple Diamond game by adding an elaborate bonus setup in a top box depicting a giant cheeseburger. Once it is triggered, the bonus round continues accumulating credits until the player hits a collect symbol or gets through all three levels of the sandwich. This reel spinner includes both multiplying wild symbols and nudge symbols. Being an option-buy (buy-a-pay) game, three coins must be bet to qualify for the top payout as well as for the secondary bonus of 2,500 coins.

DOUBLE TROUBLE

Manufacturer:	Bally Technologies
Game Format:	Reel spinner, true multiplier
Number of Reels:	3
Number of Paylines:	1
Denominations:	Nickel, quarter, or dollar
Maximum Bet:	2 coins
Top Payout:	1600 coins
Average Hit Frequency:	12%
Long-term Payback Range:	87% to 97%

A three-reel true multiplier that comes in only a two-coin version, and has multiplying wild symbols. Even with the low hit frequency, it's a perfect game for a novice.

EGYPTIAN PRINCE

Manufacturer:	Konami Gaming
Game Format:	Bonus video
Number of Reels:	5
Number of Paylines:	1-20
Denominations:	All denominations from penny to $5
Maximum Bet:	100 to 1,000 credits
Top Payout:	Line bet times 2,000 credits
Average Hit Frequency:	40% (all lines active)
Long-term Payback Range:	90%

Although it's available as a $5 slot, in most casinos, this is a penny or two-cents game. Three, four, or five scatter bonus symbols start 8, 15, or 25 free spins, respectively. During free spins, all jackpots pay double, and the free-spin round can be retriggered. Five scarab symbols on a payline will start the other bonus event, during which a special set of reels appears for two feature spins and an average bonus award of 377 credits times the total wager.

18-REELER

Manufacturer:	International Game Technology
Game Format:	Bonus video
Number of Reels:	18 (5-reel visual)
Number of Paylines:	1-40
Denomination:	Penny
Maximum Bet:	360 credits
Top Payout:	3,600,000 credits
Average Hit Frequency:	50% (all lines active)
Long-term Payback Range:	85% to 98%

The top box shows a head-on view of an 18-wheeler with the driver and his girlfriend looking through the windshield. In the five-by-four display grid, 18 of the 20 spots act as individual reels (hence, 18-reeler) along with 40 paylines. Five trucker symbols on a payline starts the main bonus sequence, in which bonus amounts in the top box grid begin to flash, stopping randomly and multiplying that amount by the line bet. This repeats as long as it keeps stopping on a different number, multiplying the result to the previous amount. The sequence ends when the flashing stops on a duplicate amount.

ELVIS (reel)

Manufacturer:	International Game Technology
Game Format:	Reel spinner, progressive
Number of Reels:	3
Number of Paylines:	1
Denomination:	Quarter
Maximum Bet:	3 coins
Top Payout:	Progressive
Progressive Reset:	$100,000
Average Hit Frequency:	9.5%
Long-term Payback:	94%

With a theme based on Elvis Presley, this MegaJackpots game includes Elvis video images and favorite tunes, enhanced by bonus awards in the LCD top-box display. The progressive jackpot resets at $100,000 and pays out in a lump sum.

ELVIS MULTI-STRIKE (video)

Manufacturer:	International Game Technology
Game Format:	Bonus video, progressive
Number of Reels:	5
Number of Paylines:	1-20
Denomination:	Penny
Maximum Bet:	300 credits
Top Payout:	Progressive
Progressive Reset:	$1 million
Average Hit Frequency:	50% (all lines active)
Long-term Payback:	88%

This version of the Elvis-themed MegaJackpots wide-area progressive has three separate sets of five-reel screens. It takes 100 coins to activate each set of reels for a 300 coin maximum wager. In addition, there are four separate bonus events. The progressive is won by lining up the letters E-L-V-I-S on the first payline of the bottom reel set. Lining up those letters on any other payline pays 3 million coins ($30,000) for a 300-coin bet.

FABULOUS 7s

Manufacturer:	Bally Technologies
Game Format:	Reel spinner, multiplier
Number of Reels:	3
Number of Paylines:	1
Denominations:	All denominations from nickel to dollar
Maximum Bet:	2, 3, or 5 coins
Top Payout (2-coin version):	5,000 coins
Top Payout (3-coin version):	7,500 coins
Top Payout (5-coin version):	12,500 coins
Average Hit Frequency:	12% to 13%
Long-term Payback Range:	88% to 97%

A three-reel spinning multiplier that comes in two-, three-, and five-coin versions and utilizes multiplying wild symbols. One Fabulous 7 symbol in a winning combination triples the payout, two multiply the payout by nine, and three on a payline, along with a maximum wager, wins the top jackpot.

FAMILY FEUD

Manufacturer:	International Game Technology
Game Format:	Bonus video or progressive
Number of Reels:	5
Number of Paylines:	1-15
Denominations:	$1, $2, or $5
Maximum Bet:	75 coins
Top Payout (non-progressive):	200,000 coins
Progressive Reset (multisite):	$500,000
Average Hit Frequency:	50% (all lines active)
Long-term Payback Range:	88% to 93%

Richard Dawson, the original host of Family Feud, is featured in this game. All the voice-overs are done by Dawson, and the game comes as a non-progressive as well as a MegaJackpots multisite progressive. The bonus round recreates the survey portion of the game show, with the player getting amounts related to the rank of the on-screen family's answers. With a maximum wager, five Family Feud logo symbols on a payline wins the progressive amount or the top jackpot in the non-progressive version.

50 LIONS

Manufacturer:	Aristocrat Technologies
Game Format:	Bonus video
Number of Reels:	5
Number of Paylines:	2-50
Denominations:	Penny, two cents, or nickel
Maximum Bet:	1,000 credits
Top Payout:	1 million credits
Average Hit Frequency:	50% to 70% (all lines active)
Long-term Payback Range:	88% to 97%

This video game with a king-of-the-jungle theme has a five-by-four symbol grid (most video games are five-by-three). Although the game has 50 paylines, each credit buys two paylines. The bonus round results in up to 15 free spins and for each spin there are more than 2,000 possible winning combinations. In the penny version, the top jackpot of one million credits amounts to $10,000.

A FISTFUL OF DOLLARS

Manufacturer:	WMS Gaming
Game Format:	Bonus video, progressive
Number of Reels:	5
Number of Paylines:	1-15
Denominations:	Nickel
Maximum Bet:	45 + 1
Top Payout:	Progressive
Progressive Reset:	$250,000
Average Hit Frequency:	41% (all lines active)
Long-term Payback Range:	89%

A spaghetti western theme, with voice-overs done by Clint Eastwood. To activate the scatter progressive and scatter bonus, as well as the main progressive jackpot, the player must wager one additional coin. Be sure to press the 15 lines + 1 button to take full advantage of these features. There are also two main bonus events. The high card bonus is activated by three scattered card symbols, and the other bonus is triggered by a wild shot symbol on the first reel.

FIVE DRAGONS

Manufacturer:	Aristocrat Technologies
Game Format:	Bonus video
Number of Reels:	5
Number of Paylines:	Scatter pay
Denominations:	All denominations from penny to dollar
Maximum Bet:	500 credits
Top Payout:	300,000 credits
Average Hit Frequency:	70% (all reels active)
Long-term Payback Range:	88% to 97%

Instead of activating paylines, in this game the player pays to activate reels, and the wins are based on scatter symbols. With all reels activated, every spin has 243 possible winning combinations. Triggering the secondary screen starts a special free-spin bonus round with up to 20 free spins and up to a 30X jackpot multiplier. The free spin bonus can be won again within the free bonus feature.

FIVE TIMES PAY (reel)

Manufacturer:	International Game Technology
Game Format:	Reel spinner, modified multiplier
Number of Reels:	3
Number of Paylines:	1
Denominations:	All or multidenominational
Maximum Bet:	1, 2, or 3 coins
Top Payout:	2,000 to 15,000 coins (set by casino)
Average Hit Frequency:	16%
Long-term Payback Range:	85% to 98%

A three-reel modified multiplier that has 5X substitute multiplier symbols to add a little excitement.

FIVE TIMES PAY (video)

Manufacturer:	International Game Technology
Game Format:	Video, reel emulator
Number of Reels:	3
Number of Paylines:	1-9
Denominations:	All or multidenominational
Maximum Bet:	180 credits
Top Payout:	10,000 credits
Average Hit Frequency:	27% (all lines active)
Long-term Payback Range:	85% to 98%

Similar to the reel spinner version with a better hit frequency and the opportunity to bet a whole lot more money.

FORT KNOX

Cleopatra	Frog Prince II
Enchanted Unicorn	Lobstermania

Manufacturer:	International Game Technology
Game Format:	Bonus video, progressive
Number of Reels:	5
Number of Paylines:	1-25 or 1-30
Denomination:	Penny
Maximum Bet (25-line version):	500 credits
Maximum Bet (30-line version):	600 credits
Top Payout:	Progressive
Platinum Reset:	$1,000 to $2,000 (casino's choice)
Gold Reset:	$100 to $200 (casino's choice)
Silver Reset:	$10 to $20 (casino's choice)
Bronze Reset:	$5 to $10 (casino's choice)
Average Hit Frequency:	50% (all lines active)
Long-term Payback:	87% to 95%

This is a bank of local progressives that pay out in a lump sum. The individual machines are popular IGT video games, each with its own unique bonus features in addition to the progressive award. Above the bank of machines is a large video monitor that displays four levels of progressive payouts which are randomly sent to one of the active games in the bank. As usual, you must bet the maximum to qualify for the progressive jackpot, and even though these are penny machines, it will cost you $5.00 a spin.

FOUNTAIN OF YOUTH

Manufacturer:	Atronic Americas
Game Format:	Bonus video
Number of Reels:	5
Number of Paylines:	1-9 or 1-21
Denominations:	All denominations
Maximum Bet:	27, 90, 210, or 525 credits
Top Payout (9-line, 27-credit version):	15,000 credits
Top Payout (9-line, 90-credit version):	50,000 credits
Top Payout (21-line, 210-credit version):	100,000 credits
Top Payout (21-line, 525-credit version):	250,000 credits
Average Hit Frequency (9-line):	31% (all lines active)
Average Hit Frequency (21-line):	34% (all lines active)
Long-term Payback Range:	86% to 96%

The main wild symbol in the primary game is a beautiful young woman. The bonus event is triggered by three or more scatter symbols, the fountain of youth. This results in 10, 15, or 25 free spins, depending on the number of scatter symbols. The player is prompted to pick a symbol of youth, and this becomes a wild symbol when the free spins occur. During the free spins, three or more scatter symbols will start an additional free-spin round.

FRENCH QUARTERS

Manufacturer:	Bally Technologies
Game Format:	Reel spinner, line game
Number of Reels:	3
Number of Paylines:	3 or 5
Denomination:	Quarter
Maximum Bet:	3 or 5 coins
Top Payout (3-line version):	40,000 coins
Top Payout (5-line version):	50,000 coins
Average Hit Frequency:	17% to 19% (all lines active)
Long-term Payback Range:	84% to 93%

A three-reel line game that comes in three- and five-payline versions, and has a high top jackpot.

GILLIGAN'S ISLAND

Manufacturer:	International Game Technology
Game Format:	Bonus video, progressive
Number of Reels:	5
Number of Paylines:	1-30
Denomination:	Penny
Maximum Bet:	300 credits
Top Payout:	Progressive
Progressive Reset:	$20,000
Average Hit Frequency:	50% (all lines active)
Long-term Payback:	92% to 93%

You'll like this MegaJackpots progressive, which has lots of animation and real video clips of the popular 1960s situation comedy—if you don't get sick of the continuously-played theme song. Two second-screen bonus events, one of which is triggered by scatter symbols, results in extra spins and credit awards. Even though it's a penny game, you'll pay $3 a spin to qualify for the progressive, but the good payback and the excellent hit frequency compensate for the cost.

GO FOR GREEN

Manufacturer:	Aristocrat Technologies
Game Format:	Bonus video
Number of Reels:	5
Number of Paylines:	1-9 or 1-20
Denominations:	All denominations from penny to dollar
Maximum Bet (9-line version):	45, 90, or 180 credits
Maximum Bet (20-line version):	100, 200, 500, or 1,000 credits
Top Payout:	10,000, 20,000, 50,000, or 150,000 credits
Average Hit Frequency (9-line):	25% to 35% (all lines active)
Average Hit Frequency (20-line):	35% to 40% (all lines active)
Long-term Payback Range:	82% to 97%

This golf-themed video slot comes in 9-line and 20-line versions. The main bonus round is triggered when three or more scattered flag symbols appear, which results in ten free spins, during which all jackpots are doubled. After each free spin, a golf ball flies from the golf course and rolls to one of the reel symbols, transforming it to a wild symbol and doubling any resulting jackpot. This can be repeated for more free spins.

GOLDEN BEAR

Manufacturer:	Konami Gaming
Game Format:	Bonus video
Number of Reels:	5
Number of Paylines:	1-10, 1-20, 1-25, or 1-30
Denominations:	All denominations from penny to $5
Maximum Bet:	30 to 3,000 credits
Top Payout:	Line bet times 4,000 credits
Mystery Jackpot Threshold (Mini):	$100
Mystery Jackpot Threshold (Major):	$1,000
Average Hit Frequency:	25% (all lines active)
Long-term Payback Range:	90%

Three or more bonus scatter symbols will start a round of 12 free spins, during which time all jackpots are doubled and the number of wild symbols is increased. This boosts the chance of hitting the bonus again during the free spins. Most casinos will have this game in the penny or two-cents version, and some casinos order this game with the mystery progressive feature, which is awarded randomly.

GOLDEN CHARIOTS

Manufacturer:	WMS Gaming
Game Format:	Hybrid reel spinner, option-buy
Number of Reels:	5
Number of Paylines:	1-9 or 1-20
Denominations:	All denominations from penny to dollar
Top Payout:	300,000 coins
Average Hit Frequency (9-line):	23% (all lines active)
Average Hit Frequency (20-line):	42% (all lines active)
Long-term Payback Range:	90% to 92%

Three scattered bonus trigger symbols results in 15 free spins. An additional wager supercharges the Hot Hot Super Jackpot respin feature which determines the number of extra free spins and increases the frequency of the bonus feature itself. If two bonus trigger symbols appear when the bonus round is activated, all jackpots on free spins are tripled.

GOLDEN TROPHY

Manufacturer:	Atronic Americas
Game Format:	Bonus video
Number of Reels:	5
Number of Paylines:	1-9 or 1-21
Denominations:	Penny, two cents, or nickel
Maximum Bet:	27, 90, 210, or 525 credits
Top Payout (9-line, 27-credit version):	30,000 credits
Top Payout (9-line, 90-credit version):	100,000 credits
Top Payout (21-line, 210-credit version):	100,000 credits
Top Payout (21-line, 525-credit version):	250,000 credits
Average Hit Frequency (9-line):	32% (all lines active)
Average Hit Frequency (21-line):	43% (all lines active)
Long-term Payback Range:	86% to 96%

Since this game is based on a horseracing theme, it is not unexpected that the bonus feature includes a horse race. Three or more Golden Trophy symbols kick off the bonus event that prompts the player to choose one of four horses. While the horses are racing on the upper screen, the main screen begins a free-spin round that lasts until three horses cross the finish line. A bonus amount is then paid according to where the selected horse finished.

GOLDMAKER

Manufacturer:	Aristocrat Technologies
Game Format:	Bonus video
Number of Reels:	5
Number of Paylines:	1-15 or 1-25
Denominations:	Penny, two cents, or nickel
Maximum Bet (15-line version):	300 credits
Maximum Bet (25-line version):	500 credits
Top Payout:	79,950 or 501,000 credits
Average Hit Frequency:	30% (all lines active)
Long-term Payback Range:	88% to 95%

In this game, a leprechaun-like scientist mixes potions and chemicals, trying to make gold. This character is a wild symbol. Three or more scattered scale symbols trigger a bonus of 12 to 20 free spins, during which all wins are doubled. Within the bonus round, if the wild scientist appears on one or more reels, those reels are held stationary, while the others are respun one time. If three or more scale symbols appear during a free spin, a new free-spin round is added on.

GOOD FORTUNE

Manufacturer:	Aristocrat Technologies
Game Format:	Bonus video
Number of Reels:	5
Number of Paylines:	2-50
Denomination:	Penny
Maximum Bet:	125, 250, or 500 credits
Top Payout (125-credit version):	$2,500
Top Payout (250-credit version):	$5,000
Top Payout (500-credit version):	$10,000
Average Hit Frequency:	70% (all lines active)
Long-term Payback Range:	88% to 98%

If you activate all the paylines, you will win almost every spin. This costs only a quarter because you get two paylines for every penny. The theme is very oriental with an array of lucky symbols. The coin symbols are wild, and the red packet scatter symbols can trigger a free-spin bonus round in which the number of wild symbols increases to improve the chances of getting more free spins.

GREAT AFRICA

Manufacturer:	Konami Gaming
Game Format:	Bonus video
Number of Reels:	5
Number of Paylines:	1-20 or 1-30
Denominations:	All denominations from penny to $5
Maximum Bet:	2,250 credits
Top Payout:	Line bet times 10,000 credits
Average Hit Frequency:	48% (all lines active)
Long-term Payback Range:	85% to 96%

With a wide range of denominations, this game with an African jungle theme comes in a 20-line or 30-line version. The Xtra Reward bonus feature only works if the player bets at least one credit per line, plus a one-credit-per-line ante wager. Then, when the Xtra Reward symbol lands on the fifth reel, all symbols on that reel become wild. There is also a free-spin bonus that can retrigger up to 120 free spins. Some versions of this game have the mystery progressive jackpot feature.

GREAT SCOT!

Manufacturer:	WMS Gaming
Game Format:	Bonus video
Number of Reels:	5
Number of Paylines:	1-9, 1-15, or 1-20
Denominations:	Penny, nickel, quarter or multidenominational
Maximum Bet:	20, 40, 100, 180, 200, or 400 credits
Top Payout:	50,000 credits
Average Hit Frequency:	72% to 79% (all lines active)
Long-term Payback Range:	84% to 95%

The theme of this game is based on a comical, red-bearded Scotsman, and has two bonus sequences that award the player credits and multipliers. Three or more Loch Ness Monster symbols on a payline starts the second screen bonus with a picture of Loch Ness, the lake where the mythical monster lives. The player is prompted to select one of several flags that sprout from the water, resulting in bonus amounts and credit multipliers. The other bonus event has quirky Scottish characters and stereotypical Scottish humor. Note the very excellent hit frequency.

GREEN ACRES

Manufacturer:	WMS Gaming
Game Format:	Bonus video, progressive
Number of Reels:	5
Number of Paylines:	1-40
Denominations:	Penny, two cents, or nickel
Maximum Bet	
(penny and two cents):	200 credits
Maximum Bet (nickel):	100 credits
Top Payout:	Progressive
Progressive Reset (penny):	$1,000
Progressive Reset (two cents):	$2,000
Progressive Reset (nickel):	$2,500
Average Hit Frequency:	54% (all lines active)
Long-term Payback Range:	87% to 90%

This game, based on the Green Acres sitcom of the 1960s, has a five-by-five grid of reel symbols that includes an expanding wild symbol. For a minimum bet of 25 cents, you can activate all 40 paylines and get the full range of hit frequency and payback percentage that is available. Several bonus events pay varying jackpots, and are all based on scenes from the show. The top jackpot is a local-area progressive.

GRIZZLY

Manufacturer:	Aristocrat Technologies
Game Format:	Bonus video
Number of Reels:	5
Number of Paylines:	1-25
Denominations:	All denominations from penny to dollar
Maximum Bet:	125, 250, or 500 credits
Top Payout (125-credit version):	100,000 credits
Top Payout (250-credit version):	200,000 credits
Top Payout (500-credit version):	400,000 credits
Average Hit Frequency:	40% (all lines active)
Long-term Payback Range:	88% to 95%

This game is based on a fishing theme centered around a comical bear trying to catch fish. An interactive bonus round has the player trying to direct the bear in an attempt to catch fish in a stream, during which varying multipliers are earned. When the fishing trip is completed, 12 free spins are played and the wins are boosted by the earned multiplier. These wins can include additional free spins.

GYPSY FORTUNE

Manufacturer:	Atronic Americas
Game Format:	Bonus video
Number of Reels:	5
Number of Paylines:	1-9 or 1-21
Denominations:	All denominations
Maximum Bet (9-line):	27, 45, or 90 credits
Maximum Bet (21-line):	63 or 210 credits
Top Payout:	100,000 credits
Average Hit Frequency (9-line):	35% (all lines active)
Average Hit Frequency (21-line):	50% (all lines active)
Long-term Payback Range:	86% to 94%

A jackpot is awarded when two or three scatter-pay mystic moon symbols appear. Four or five mystic moon symbols trigger a bonus event in which the reels become spinning credit amounts. Two more bonus levels involve fortune-telling cards and floating jewels. The Gypsy Queen is a wild symbol, and five of them on a payline triggers the top jackpot of 100,000 credits.

HEART OF VEGAS

Manufacturer:	Aristocrat Technologies
Game Format:	Bonus video
Number of Reels:	5
Number of Paylines:	1-100 or 2-100
Denominations:	All denominations from penny to dollar
Maximum Bet:	1,000 credits
Top Payout (2-100-line version):	50,000 credits
Top Payout (1-100-line version):	100,000 credits
Average Hit Frequency:	33% (all lines active)
Long-term Payback Range:	88% to 95%

There are two 100-line versions, one of which gives two lines per credit, so 50 cents on the penny slot gets all 100 paylines. The bonus round of ten free spins is started by three scattered Welcome to Las Vegas sign symbols. With each spin, a wild heart symbol is added to a reel and remains for all subsequent free spins, until there is a wild symbol on the second through fifth reels. These wild symbols then remain for the following five spins.

HEE HAW

Manufacturer:	Bally Technologies
Game Format:	Bonus reel spinner, progressive
Number of Reels:	5
Number of Paylines:	1-9
Denominations:	Penny
Maximum Bet:	90 coins
Top Payout:	Progressive
Top Progressive Reset:	$2,500
Other Progressive Resets:	$10, $50, $100, and $1,000
Average Hit Frequency:	33% (all lines active)
Long-term Payback Range:	88% to 96%

The long-running country music and comedy TV show is the theme of this reel spinner, which acts more like a bonus video slot. The video top box displays five progressive amounts that can be won with ears of corn on an active payline with maximum coins. Certain scatter symbols activate a free-spin round, during which the top box screen changes to show animated characters from the Hee Haw show.

HIGHWAY 777

Manufacturer:	Konami Gaming
Game Format:	Reel spinner, option-buy
Number of Reels:	4
Number of Paylines:	1
Denominations:	Nickel, quarter, half, dollar, $2, or $5
Maximum Bet:	3 coins
Top Payout:	10,000 coins
Average Hit Frequency:	16%
Long-term Payback Range:	87% to 98%

This is actually a three-reel machine where the fourth reel is an LCD screen that displays bonus features that are applied to winning combinations. The bonus reel contains 2X, 5X, and 10X multipliers, a respin, and a mystery bonus. The mystery bonus awards a random amount that ranges from 10 credits to 500 credits. Of course, since this is an option-buy (buy-a-pay) game, the bonus reel is only active for a maximum wager.

HOLLYWOOD SQUARES – PREMIER NIGHT

Manufacturer:	WMS Gaming
Game Format:	Bonus video
Number of Reels:	5
Number of Paylines:	1-9, 1-15, or 1-20
Denominations:	All denominations from penny to $25
Maximum Bet (9-line version):	45, 90, or 180
Maximum Bet (15-line version):	75, 50, or 300
Maximum Bet (20-line version):	100, 200, or 400
Top Payout:	50,000 credits
Average Hit Frequency:	40% to 49% (all lines active)
Long-term Payback Range:	86% to 93%

Another in the Hollywood Squares series, this has an elaborate top-box display and three separate bonus events, each of which awards extra credits. The main bonus changes the video screen into a giant tic-tac-toe board and a live video of Joan Rivers. Older versions of Hollywood Squares, such as Prize Spin, The Center Square, and Tour of Stars have fewer payline choices. The game has a nice hit frequency and comes in a very wide range of denominations.

HOUDINI

Manufacturer:	WMS Gaming
Game Format:	Bonus video
Number of Reels:	5
Number of Paylines:	1-30
Denominations:	Penny, two cents, or nickel
Maximum Bet:	600 credits
Top Payout:	30,000 credits
Average Hit Frequency:	35% (all lines active)
Long-term Payback Range:	86% to 94%

Instead of reels, this game has circular symbols arranged in three rows of five, four, and five. Normally, these symbols behave like regular reel symbols and pay off when the correct combination falls on a payline. However, when a Rotating Wild symbol lands on one of the two middle circles in the center row, the six symbols surrounding the wild symbol rotate until they form a new payline combination. This continues until the circle of symbols makes a complete rotation, paying off for each win that hits. If both middle symbols are wild, then many more payouts result. There is also a second screen free-spin bonus event.

THE HOUSE OF THE DEAD EX

Manufacturer:	International Game Technology
Game Format:	Bonus video
Number of Reels:	5
Number of Paylines:	Scatter pay
Denominations:	Penny
Maximum Bet:	1,250 credits
Top Payout:	250,000 credits
Average Hit Frequency:	23% (all reels active)
Long-term Payback Range:	85% to 98%

Instead of activating paylines, in this horror-themed game the player pays to activate the reels. With a three-by-five matrix, there are actually fifteen reels because each of the symbols spins independently—so it costs at least fifteen credits to activate all of them. All wins are based on scatter symbols, and with all reels activated, every spin has 243 possible winning combinations.

I DREAM OF JEANNIE MAGIC SPIN

Manufacturer:	International Game Technology
Game Format:	Bonus video, progressive
Number of Reels:	5
Number of Paylines:	1-15
Denominations:	Penny or nickel
Maximum Bet (penny version):	150 credits
Maximum Bet (nickel version):	75 credits
Top Payout:	Progressive
Progressive Reset:	$100,000
Average Hit Frequency:	50% (all lines active)
Long-term Payback Range:	88% to 90%

The Jeannie theme is augmented with a voice-over by Barbara Eden. This is a good MegaJackpots progressive with a high hit frequency even though the penny version costs only $1.50 for a spin. The progressive award is paid as a lump sum. Three or more bonus symbols start the Magic Spin Bonus event, during which the player is prompted to pick a genie bottle. This causes the bonus wheel to spin until it awards an amount that may be from 15 to 1,000 times the line bet. The chosen bottle may reveal an additional multiplier.

JACKPOT SLUGGER

Manufacturer:	Konami Gaming
Game Format:	Bonus reel spinner
Number of Reels:	3
Number of Paylines:	1
Denominations:	All denominations from quarter to $25
Maximum Bet:	3 coins
Top Payout:	2,000 coins
Average Hit Frequency:	19%
Long-term Payback:	97%

Based on a baseball theme, this game has both spinning reels and a video display. As the reels spin, the bonus screen shows a pitcher throwing to a batter. Whenever a winning combination occurs on the reels, the batter hits the ball into a spot that determines the award. A second bonus screen is based on how far the batter hits the ball. Three Hit symbols on the payline start a free-spin bonus with four winning combinations. Since the long-term payback is high, this machine will mainly be found in the higher denominations.

JEFF FOXWORTHY – YOU MIGHT BE A REDNECK IF . . .

Manufacturer:	Aristocrat Technologies
Game Format:	Bonus video
Number of Reels:	5
Number of Paylines:	1-20
Denominations:	Penny, two cents, nickel, or quarter
Maximum Bet:	125, 250, 500, or 1,000 credits
Top Payout (125-credit version):	250,000 credits
Top Payout (250-credit version):	500,000 credits
Top Payout (500-credit version):	1 million credits
Top Payout (1,000-credit version):	2 million credits
Average Hit Frequency:	50% (all lines active)
Long-term Payback Range:	81% to 92%

Based on Jeff Foxworthy's comedy routines, this machine has low volatility and five different second-screen bonus games. The five games are: Bug Zapper, Christmas Lights, Pick a TV, Pig Bonus, and Squirrel Pie. In order to activate the bonus features, however, the player has to wager an additional five credits per payline. In the primary game, the Pig is a scatter-pay symbol, and the Moonshine symbol in the middle reels is wild.

JEOPARDY!

Manufacturer:	International Game Technology
Game Format:	Reel spinner, progressive
Number of Reels:	3
Number of Paylines:	1
Denomination:	Quarter
Maximum Bet:	3 coins
Top Payout:	Progressive
Progressive Reset:	$200,000
Average Hit Frequency:	12%
Long-term Payback:	93%

The Jeopardy theme features great visual and sound effects in this MegaJackpots multisite progressive. When the Jeopardy or Double Jeopardy symbol stops on the payline, the player can press the Play Jeopardy button causing lights to flash on the bonus board and win up to 2,000 credits. Since this is a quarter machine, qualifying for the progressive costs only 75 cents a spin. Fifty cents and dollar versions are also available in Atlantic City. Some of the base games with the Jeopardy theme are White Ice, Triple Lucky 7's, Double Diamond, Triple Diamond, Five Times Pay, and Ten Times Pay.

JOHNNY VEGAS

Manufacturer:	Atronic Americas
Game Format:	Bonus video
Number of Reels:	5
Number of Paylines:	1-9 or 1-21
Denominations:	Penny, two cents, or nickel
Maximum Bet:	27, 90, 210, or 525 credits
Top Payout (9-line, 27-credit version):	15,000 credits
Top Payout (9-line, 90-credit version):	50,000 credits
Top Payout (21-line, 210-credit version):	100,000 credits
Top Payout (21-line, 525-credit version):	250,000 credits
Average Hit Frequency (9-line):	37% (all lines active)
Average Hit Frequency (21-line):	46% (all lines active)
Long-term Payback Range:	86% to 94%

The Johnny Vegas symbol is wild for all but the bonus sign, which is a scatter symbol. When three bonus sign symbols land anywhere on reels 1, 3, and 5, the player is awarded 10 free spins. During those free spins, the bonus signs are also wild which increases the chances of retriggering the free spin feature during a free spin.

THE JOKER'S WILD

Manufacturer:	International Game Technology
Game Format:	Reel spinner, option-buy, progressive
Number of Reels:	3
Number of Paylines:	5
Denomination:	Quarter
Maximum Bet:	5 coins
Top Payout:	Progressive
Progressive Reset:	$100,000
Average Hit Frequency:	17% (all lines active)
Long-term Payback Range:	87% to 90%

This MegaJackpots progressive is fitted with a top box bonus game that has the giant reels popularized on the old TV game show. The bonus begins when three bonus symbols appear on any active payline. The player is prompted to press the spin button to start the bonus reels, and they continue to spin until a devil symbol lands on the payline of the bonus reels. Lining up three 3X symbols on the center payline with a maximum bet wins the MegaJackpots progressive.

LIFE OF LUXURY

Far East Fortunes
Jungle Cats
Riches of Rome

Manufacturer:	WMS Gaming
Game Format:	Bonus video, progressive
Number of Reels:	5
Number of Paylines:	1-20 or 1-30
Denominations:	Penny, two cents, or nickel
Maximum Bet	
(penny and two cents):	240 credits
Maximum Bet (nickel):	100 credits
Top Payout:	Progressive
Top Progressive Reset (penny):	$1,000
Top Progressive Reset (two cents):	$2,000
Top Progressive Reset (nickel):	$5,000
Average Hit Frequency:	40% (all lines active)
Long-term Payback Range:	87% to 96%

This is a bank of progressive machines with three different base games under a large display showing five progressive jackpots. The jackpots are identified by different gems, the top award being the diamond. When a gem symbol lands on the correct reel, a bonus screen appears and the player may get a credit award or the progressive jackpot for that gem. If the player had bet the maximum, the progressive is automatically won. The three games are all mathematically similar, but have different bonus events.

LI'L LUCY

Deviled Eggs   Wild Panthers
Flamin' Fortune

Manufacturer:	Aristocrat Technologies
Game Format:	Bonus video, linked
Number of Reels:	5
Number of Paylines:	1-20
Denominations:	Penny, two cents, or nickel
Maximum Bet:	150, 300, 600, or 1,200 credits
Top Payout (150-credit version):	250,000 credits
Top Payout (300-credit version):	500,000 credits
Top Payout (600-credit version):	1 million credits
Top Payout (1,200-credit version):	2 million credits
Average Hit Frequency:	50% (all lines active)
Long-term Payback Range:	81% to 93%

These games have four versions with top payouts ranging from 250,000 to 2 million credits. When play reaches a predetermined coin-in range, random bonus events occur in all machines in a linked group. The more people playing in the group, the more often the bonus events occur. Thus, if you can find a bank of machines that is almost full, you are in for some exciting play and some good wins. However, to qualify for any of the five different bonus events, the player must make an ante bet in addition to the line bet.

LOCO LOOT

Choy Sun Doa   Red Baron
Pompeii   Whales of Cash

Manufacturer:	Aristocrat Technologies
Game Format:	Bonus video, linked progressive
Number of Reels:	5
Number of Paylines:	Scatter pay
Denomination:	Penny
Maximum Bet:	500 credits
Top Payout:	Progressive
Progressive Reset (Grand):	$10,000
Progressive Reset (Major):	$150
Progressive Reset (Minor):	$15
Progressive Reset (Mini):	$5
Average Hit Frequency:	70% (all reels active)
Long-term Payback Range:	88%

This is a bank of progressive machines with four different base games under a large locomotive display showing four progressive jackpots. In these games the player pays to activate reels instead of paylines; in fact, there are no paylines. All wins are based on scatter symbols with a very high hit frequency. For maximum success, the games should be played with all reels activated. Although a small wager will eventually result in a bonus event, the larger the wager, the faster the bonus rounds will occur.

LOVE BIRDS

Manufacturer:	Aristocrat Technologies
Game Format:	Bonus video
Number of Reels:	5
Number of Paylines:	1-9 or 1-20
Denominations:	All denominations from penny to dollar
Maximum Bet (9-line version):	45 to 180 credits
Maximum Bet (20-line version):	100 to 1,000 credits
Top Payouts:	50,000, 100,000, or 200,000 credits
Average Hit Frequency:	50% (all lines active)
Long-term Payback Range:	88% to 95%

The blue and pink love bird characters are wild symbols. When two or more appear scattered anywhere on the reels, they trigger the free-spin bonus. Any combination of two to five scattered birds results in 5 to 50 free spins with all wins doubled. If two or more love birds appear during a free spin, the bonus round is repeated with more free spins added to the total.

LUAU PARTY

Manufacturer:	Bally Technologies
Game Format:	Bonus video
Number of Reels:	5
Number of Paylines:	1-15
Denominations:	All denominations from penny to dollar
Maximum Bet:	450 credits
Top Payout:	50,000 credits
Average Hit Frequency:	36% (all lines active)
Long-term Payback Range:	88% to 96%

This is a standard 15-line video game with a bonus round that gives out 15 free spins, during which time all the winning jackpots pay triple. More free spins can be triggered during the bonus round.

MAGIC 8 BALL

Manufacturer:	International Game Technology
Game Format:	Bonus video, progressive
Number of Reels:	5
Number of Paylines:	1-15
Denomination:	Nickel
Maximum Bet:	75 credits
Top Payout:	Progressive
Progressive Reset:	$100,000
Average Hit Frequency:	50% (all lines active)
Long-term Payback:	89%

This is a MegaJackpots multisite progressive with a very high hit frequency. It is a low-volatility game with a bonus event that results in free spins that play out automatically and bonus amounts up to 1,000 credits. As usual, you must bet the maximum to qualify for the progressive jackpot that pays out in a lump sum. Even though this is a nickel machine, it will cost you $3.75 a spin.

MEGABUCKS (reel)

Manufacturer:	International Game Technology
Game Format:	Reel spinner, progressive
Number of Reels:	3 or 4
Number of Paylines:	1
Denomination:	Dollar
Maximum Bet:	2 or 3 coins
Top Payout:	Progressive
Progressive Reset:	$10 million in Nevada
Long-term Payback:	86% before progressive

Megabucks machines may be found in most casinos within each major gambling jurisdiction such as Nevada and Mississippi, as well as in tribal casinos. All the machines in a given jurisdiction are linked to the same huge jackpot pool. Megabucks may be a three- or four-reel machine, and depending on the location, it may have a two- or three-coin maximum bet, so you have to invest $2 or $3 on each spin to qualify for the progressive jackpot. Line up the three (or four) Megabucks symbols on the payline and you win a multimillion dollar jackpot that is paid out in 25 annual installments. In Nevada, the jackpot reset is $10 million. In other jurisdictions, the reset is usually lower. For reasons not fully understood, the Megabucks network never succeeded in New Jersey, and the machines were eventually removed.

MEGABUCKS (video)

Manufacturer:	International Game Technology
Game Format:	Bonus video, progressive
Number of Reels:	5
Number of Paylines:	1- 60
Denomination:	Penny
Maximum Bet:	300 credits
Top Payout:	Progressive
Progressive Reset:	$10 million in Nevada
Average Hit Frequency:	50% (all lines active)
Long-term Payback:	90%

This is the video version of the famous Megabucks multisite progressive network. It has two bonus features and low volatility, but the odds of hitting the progressive are almost twice as tough as the traditional Megabucks dollar reel spinner. Besides the high hit frequency, this game has two bonus events with award multipliers of up to 5X the line bet. Even though it is a penny machine, to win the progressive, you still have to make a maximum bet of $3.00.

MIAMI VICE

Manufacturer:	Atronic Americas
Game Format:	Bonus video, progressive
Number of Reels:	5
Number of Paylines:	1-21
Denomination:	Penny
Maximum Bet:	210 or 525 credits
Top Payout:	Progressive
Progressive Reset (210-credit version):	$5,250
Progressive Reset (525-credit version):	$13,125
Average Hit Frequency:	38% (all lines active)
Long-term Payback Range:	86% to 96%

This is a stand-alone progressive with the theme of the 1980s cop show. The letters M, I, A, M, and I are scatter symbols, three or four of which trigger a multilevel second-screen bonus event that accumulates credits from various player choices. With a maximum wager, all five of the letters win the progressive amount.

MILLIONAIRE SEVENS

Manufacturer:	Bally Technologies
Game Format:	Bonus video, progressive
Number of Reels:	5
Number of Paylines:	1-20 or 1-30
Denomination:	Penny or nickel
Maximum Bet (penny):	300 credits
Maximum Bet (nickel):	60 credits
Top Payout:	Progressive
Progressive Reset:	$1 million
Average Hit Frequency (penny):	45% (all lines active)
Average Hit Frequency (nickel):	36% (all lines active)
Long-term Payback Range:	87% to 88%

Scattered Millionaire Sevens symbols start the bonus sequence in this multisite progressive game. The player selects a face-down card that advances one to three steps on the top-box bonus ladder which has multiplier amounts from 2X to 500X. The amounts are multiplied by the total bet to arrive at the payout. This continues until the player turns a card with a Collect symbol or reaches the progressive rung. At less than a maximum bet, the progressive rung pays 1,000 times the total bet.

MONEY GARDEN

Manufacturer:	Bally Technologies
Game Format:	Bonus video
Number of Reels:	5
Number of Paylines:	1-15
Denominations:	Nickel, quarter, half, dollar, or $5
Maximum Bet:	450 credits
Top Payout:	Line bet times 10,000 credits
Average Hit Frequency:	12% (all lines active)
Long-term Payback Range:	88% to 96%

This is a standard five-reel, 15-line video game with a maximum bet of 30 credits per line. The bonus round is triggered by three or more butterfly symbols and gives the player 15 free spins, during which time all the winning jackpots pay three times as much. This can go on for as many as 49 free spins.

MONEY HONEY

Wizard Ways

Manufacturer:	Aristocrat Technologies
Game Format:	Bonus video, linked
Number of Reels:	5
Number of Paylines:	Scatter pay
Denominations:	Penny, two cents, or nickel
Maximum Bet:	175 or 350 credits
Top Payout (175-credit version):	350,000 credits
Top Payout (350-credit version):	700,000 credits
Average Hit Frequency:	50% (all reels active)
Long-term Payback Range:	88% to 92%

These games have two versions with top payouts of 350,000 and 700,000 credits. There are no paylines, and all wins are based on scatter symbols. To qualify for the main set of bonus rounds, which include free spins, the player must activate all reels and add an ante wager of 10 credits. With all reels activated, every spin has 243 possible winning combinations. A bank of machines with many players will result in more frequent bonus events.

MONEY MATCH

Manufacturer:	Bally Technologies
Game Format:	Bonus reel spinner, option-buy
Number of Reels:	3
Number of Paylines:	1
Denominations:	Quarter, half, or dollar
Maximum Bet:	3 coins
Top Payout:	4,000 coins
Average Hit Frequency:	29% to 32%
Long-term Payback Range:	90% to 97%

Three Money Match symbols lined up on the reel spinner payline starts the bonus game on the video screen. The player is prompted to select one of twelve Money Match icons which partially reveals bonus amounts. The player continues to select icons until a match is found and then is awarded the bonus. Three Super Jackpot symbols gets the top jackpot of 4,000 coins, provided the player wagered the maximum bet of three coins.

MONEY MONEY

Manufacturer:	Bally Technologies
Game Format:	Bonus video
Number of Reels:	5
Number of Paylines:	1-25
Denomination:	Penny
Maximum Bet:	1,250 credits
Top Payout:	Line bet times 100,000 credits
Average Hit Frequency:	36% (all lines active)
Long-term Payback Range:	88% to 96%

This game is loaded with wild symbol multipliers: 2X, 3X, 5X and/or 10X. Besides being wild, the symbols multiply the jackpots in winning combinations. If more than one of the wild symbols fall on a payline, they multiply together, which can result in a large credit win.

MONOPOLY – CASH FLOW

Manufacturer:	WMS Gaming
Game Format:	Bonus video
Number of Reels:	5
Number of Paylines:	1-9 or 1-15
Denominations:	All denominations from nickel to $25
Maximum Bet (9-line):	45 or 90 credits
Maximum Bet (15-line):	75 or 150 credits
Top Payout:	50,000 credits
Average Hit Frequency:	28% to 31% (all lines active)
Long-term Payback Range:	89% to 93%

Cash Flow comes in either a 9-line or 15-line version of Monopoly with three bonus events. The bonus awards result in either a win multiplier, a line wager multiplier, or free spins, during which the properties increase in value. When playing the free spins, the best plan is to accumulate as many properties as possible.

MONOPOLY – HOT PROPERTIES

Manufacturer:	WMS Gaming
Game Format:	Bonus video
Number of Reels:	5
Number of Paylines:	1-9
Denominations:	Nickel, quarter, or dollar
Maximum Bet:	9, 18, 45, or 90 credits
Top Payout:	50,000 credits
Average Hit Frequency:	41% (all lines active)
Long-term Payback Range:	88% to 94%

Another in the popular Monopoly series, this version is based on buying real estate. It is a basic 9-line video with four separate bonus events. One of them depicts a race between four trains for which the player has to try to pick the winner. Another is the Hat Bonus in which the player selects from a group of hats sitting on a table in front of Mr. Monopoly. With all nine lines bet, the hit frequency is not bad.

MONOPOLY MONEY – WILD CHANCE

Manufacturer:	WMS Gaming
Game Format:	Reel spinner, progressive
Number of Reels:	3
Number of Paylines:	1
Denominations:	Quarter or dollar
Maximum Bet:	3 coins
Top Payout:	Progressive
Progressive Reset:	$250,000 in Nevada
Average Hit Frequency:	14%
Long-term Payback Range:	88% to 90%

WMS used the Monopoly theme to kick off its first multisite progressive, which pays in one lump sum. It features multiplying symbols and a top box bonus round. When a Monopoly Money symbol lands on the third reel with three coins bet, the top box bonus sequence is triggered with awards ranging up to 1,000 coins, which can be doubled by landing on Chance, or tripled by landing on Community Chest. Three Monopoly logo symbols on the payline win the progressive award. In some jurisdictions outside of Nevada, the reset may be as low as $100,000.

MONOPOLY – PARTY TRAIN

Manufacturer:	WMS Gaming
Game Format:	Bonus video, progressive
Number of Reels:	5
Number of Paylines:	1-20 or 1-25
Denominations:	Penny or nickel
Maximum Bet (20-line, nickel version):	200
Maximum Bet (25-line, penny version):	80
Top Payout:	Progressive
Progressive Reset (multisite):	$100,000
Progressive Reset (local):	$500 (penny) or $1,000 (nickel)
Average Hit Frequency:	47% to 55% (all lines active)
Long-term Payback Range:	88%

This Monopoly progressive has a multisite award as well as a local award. It comes in a 25-line penny version and a 20-line nickel version. A Chance card symbol on the fifth reel awards a credit amount, a bonus multiplier, or entry into the Mrs. Monopoly Pick

'N Match bonus. The Mrs. Monopoly bonus allows the player to select hidden properties, and if a color group is matched, extra picks are awarded on a path to the local progressive jackpot. The multisite progressive is won by lining up five Monopoly Progressive symbols.

MONOPOLY – SUPER GRAND HOTEL

Manufacturer:	WMS Gaming
Game Format:	Bonus video
Number of Reels:	5
Number of Paylines:	1-15, 1-20, or 1-25
Denominations:	All denominations
Maximum Bet (15-line):	150 credits
Maximum Bet (20-line):	200 credits
Maximum Bet (25-line):	250 credits
Top Payout:	Line bet times 50,000 credits
Average Hit Frequency:	45% (all lines active)
Long-term Payback Range:	86% to 96%

This is a new version of the Grand Hotel. Three or more scattered elevator symbols start the top-box bonus, and the player gets six to ten free spins. During the free spins, three or more Going Up arrows on a payline cause the center arrows to flash upward and stop at one of the six floors for a bonus credit. In the other bonus sequence, the screen transforms into a Monopoly board and the player selects a railroad and five properties on which to place hotels. As property values increase, so do the credit awards.

MONTY PYTHON AND THE HOLY GRAIL

Manufacturer:	International Game Technology
Game Format:	Bonus video, progressive
Number of Reels:	5
Number of Paylines:	1-15
Denomination:	Nickel
Maximum Bet:	75 credits
Top Payout:	Progressive
Progressive Reset:	$100,000
Average Hit Frequency:	50% (all lines active)
Long-term Payback Range:	88% to 90%

Bet 75 credits and get five Holy Grail symbols on the first payline of this MegaJackpots game, and you'll be paid the progressive jackpot in a lump sum. Three Holy Grail symbols on an active payline starts a multilevel bonus sequence in which the player gets seven spins of the die in the top box, representing seven moves around the game board to collect mystery credit amounts. There are many other bonus events involving either a second screen or the top box. Holy Grail fans will not be disappointed.

MOON FESTIVAL

Manufacturer:	Aristocrat Technologies
Game Format:	Bonus video
Number of Reels:	5
Number of Paylines:	1-50 or 2-50
Denominations:	All denominations from penny to dollar
Maximum Bet (1-50 paylines):	250, 500, or 1,000 credits
Maximum Bet (2-50 paylines):	125, 250, or 500 credits
Top Payout (125/250-credit version):	25,000 credits
Top Payout (250/500-credit version):	50,000 credits
Top Payout (500/1,000-credit version):	100,000 credits
Average Hit Frequency:	59% (all lines active)
Long-term Payback Range:	88% to 95%

As can be seen above, there are two 50-line versions, one of which gives two lines per credit, so a quarter on the penny slot gets all 50 paylines. The bonus round of ten free spins is started by three scattered lantern symbols. During the free spins, whenever a moon symbol appears, it becomes wild and remains frozen in place for the remainder of the free spins. If the bonus is retriggered during the free spins, the wild symbols remain in place for the entire round.

MYSTERY II

Manufacturer:	Atronic Americas
Game Format:	Bonus video
Number of Reels:	5
Number of Paylines:	1-9 or 1-21
Denominations:	All denominations
Maximum Bet:	27, 90, 210, or 525 credits
Top Payout (9-line, 27-credit version):	30,000 credits
Top Payout (9-line, 90-credit version):	100,000 credits
Top Payout (21-line, 210-credit version):	100,000 credits
Top Payout (21-line, 525-credit version):	250,000 credits
Average Hit Frequency (9-line):	30% (all lines active)
Average Hit Frequency (21-line):	39% (all lines active)
Long-term Payback Range:	86% to 94%

This Phantom of the Opera themed game has three separate bonus events. In the highest bonus level, there is an elaborate ring game in which the player starts the rings spinning by pressing a button on the screen. If the bonus ring is highlighted, the player wins more ring spins with a 2X multiplier.

MYSTIC LAMP

Manufacturer:	Bally Technologies
Game Format:	Bonus reel spinner
Number of Reels:	5
Number of Paylines:	1-30
Denominations:	Penny to dollar or multidenominational
Maximum Bet:	3,000 coins
Top Payout:	Line bet times 1,000 credits
Average Hit Frequency:	44% (all lines active)
Long-term Payback Range:	86% to 96%

This reel spinner is actually a hybrid that acts more like a bonus video slot with a video screen in the top box. Scatter symbols increase payoffs up to 200 times the total bet. A Bonus Lamp anywhere on the third reel starts the main bonus sequence. The player is prompted to select one lamp, which leads to one of three secondary bonus events that give awards from five to 170 times the total wager.

NEPTUNE'S EXPLORATION INC.

Manufacturer:	International Game Technology
Game Format:	Bonus reel spinner
Number of Reels:	5
Number of Paylines:	1-20
Denomination:	Penny
Maximum Bet:	200 coins
Top Payout:	100,000 coins ($1,000)
Average Hit Frequency:	50% (all lines active)
Long-term Payback:	85% to 94%

This is a reel spinner that behaves more like a video slot, and features an elaborate top-box bonus display. Three or more bonus symbols trigger flashing lights in the top box to display two bonus trails. When the bonus sequence begins, a die rolls to a number of spaces which flash and lead to a credit amount or a question mark. The question mark moves the trail to the upper part of the top box to collect more credits.

PEARLY GATES

Manufacturer:	Bally Technologies
Game Format:	Bonus video
Number of Reels:	5
Number of Paylines:	1-9
Denominations:	Nickel, quarter, or dollar
Maximum Bet:	9 to 270 credits, casino adjustable
Top Payout:	Line bet times 5,000 credits
Average Hit Frequency:	37% (all lines active)
Long-term Payback Range:	88% to 94%

Three Hand from Above symbols trigger the second screen bonus event, which is a funny sequence in which screen characters are judged with bonus amounts accruing for the lucky ones who go to Heaven. For those who don't make it, there is no bonus payout. Of course, the fate of these characters has already been decided by the computer's random-number generator. The amount of the top payout depends on the line bet.

PELICAN PETE

Manufacturer:	Aristocrat Technologies
Game Format:	Bonus video
Number of Reels:	5
Number of Paylines:	1-50
Denominations:	All denominations from penny to dollar
Maximum Bet:	500 credits
Top Payout:	100,000 credits
Average Hit Frequency:	60% (all lines active)
Long-term Payback Range:	88% to 95%

This game has a seafaring theme, and the 50 paylines result in a very high hit frequency. If all the paylines are active, three scattered lighthouse symbols appearing anywhere on the reels wins ten free spins. If, during the free spins, a Pelican Pete symbol appears on any reel, it freezes in place and that spot remains wild for the remaining free spins, increasing the possibility of a retrigger of the free-spin bonus.

PHOENIX GOLD

Manufacturer:	International Game Technology
Game Format:	Reel spinner, option-buy
Number of Reels:	3
Number of Paylines:	1
Denominations:	Quarter or dollar
Maximum Bet:	3 coins
Top Payout:	4,000 coins
Average Hit Frequency:	15%
Long-term Payback Range:	85% to 98%

This standard three-reel, single-payline game is spruced up with an interesting top box bonus event consisting of arrows being shot at bundles of money. The game also has 2X and 3X substitute multiplier symbols, along with the popular nudge symbols. Since this is an option-buy (buy-a-pay) game, you must bet all three coins to qualify for the bonus round.

PLAYBOY GET LUCKY WHEEL

Manufacturer:	Bally Technologies
Game Format:	Bonus video, progressive
Number of Reels:	5
Number of Paylines:	1-25
Denomination:	Penny
Maximum Bet:	125 credits
Top Payout:	Progressive
Progressive Reset:	$250,000
Average Hit Frequency:	62% (all lines active)
Long-term Payback Range:	88% to 90%

Line up five of the title symbols on an active payline and you win the top jackpot in this QuarterMillion$ wide-area progressive. Three adjacent Get Lucky Wheel symbols anywhere on the screen triggers the top-box wheel to spin. The player is prompted to press a button to stop the wheel and is paid the amounts shown by the illuminated arrows.

PLAYBOY MYSTERY PROGRESSIVE

Manufacturer:	Bally Technologies
Game Format:	Bonus video, progressive
Number of Reels:	5
Number of Paylines:	1-3, 1-5, 1-9, 1-15, 1-20, or 1-25
Denominations:	All denominations from penny to $100
Maximum Bet:	1,250 credits
Top Payout:	Line bet times 15,000 credits
Top Progressive Reset:	$1,000
Other Progressive Resets:	$5, $20, and $100
Average Hit Frequency:	28% (all lines active)
Long-term Payback Range:	88% to 96%

This is a four-level mystery progressive where the progressive awards are paid randomly. Three or more scattered Hef symbols start a free-spin bonus that awards 15 free spins, and all jackpots are tripled. During the free spins, the bonus can be triggered again. Three Playmate symbols trigger the Centerfold bonus which can result in an award of from 3 to 100 times the total wager.

POPCORN SLOTTO

Manufacturer:	AC Coin and Slot
Game Format:	Reel spinner, option-buy
Number of Reels:	3
Number of Paylines:	1 or 5
Denominations:	All denominations from quarter to $50
Maximum Bet:	3 or 5 coins
Top Payout:	2,400 coins
Average Hit Frequency (1-line version):	15%
Average Hit Frequency (5-line version):	40% (all lines active)
Long-term Payback Range:	89% to 96%

The core reel spinner is either an IGT Double Diamond three-reel, three-coin version or an IGT Triple Stars three-reel, five-line, five-coin version. To this is added a top box in the form of a popcorn popper to handle the bonus feature. When the bonus is triggered, popcorn in the form of lotto balls percolate out of the kettle with the sound effect of an actual popcorn machine, resulting in awards ranging up to 250 coins with a possible 2X multiplier. Since this is an option-buy (buy-a-pay) game, a maximum wager is needed to activate the bonus event.

THE PRICE IS RIGHT SERIES
Cliff Hangers
Dice Game
Money Game
Plinko
Punch a Bunch

Manufacturer:	International Game Technology
Game Format:	Bonus video
Number of Reels:	5
Number of Paylines:	1-15
Denominations:	Multidenominational
Maximum Bet:	75 credits
Top Payout:	200,000 credits
Average Hit Frequency:	38% (all lines active)
Long-term Payback:	85% to 94%

The advantage to the slot version of this long-running game show is that you can pick the game you like best (subject to casino availability). This game machine has been around for a while, thus the voice-over is by the late Rod Roddy. Each version has its unique bonus screens and credit awards, but always includes a Showcase Showdown bonus round.

PROPHECY

Manufacturer:	Aristocrat Technologies
Game Format:	Bonus video
Number of Reels:	5
Number of Paylines:	Scatter pay
Denominations:	All denominations from penny to dollar
Maximum Bet:	200 or 500 credits
Top Payout (200-credit version):	12,000 credits
Top Payout (500-credit version):	30,000 credits
Average Hit Frequency:	70% (all reels active)
Long-term Payback Range:	88% to 97%

All wins in this game are based on scatter symbols; there are no paylines. The player pays to activate reels instead of paylines, and with all reels activated, every spin has 243 possible winning combinations. A scattered book symbol activates a second screen feature that leads to bonus prizes. The game then automatically starts 15 free spins. During these spins, the crystal ball symbol is wild and multiplies wins by two, three, or five. During the spin event, more spins can be won.

RAIDERS OF THE LOST ARK

Manufacturer:	International Game Technology
Game Format:	Reel spinner, progressive
Number of Reels:	5
Number of Paylines:	1-9
Denomination:	Penny
Maximum Bet:	27 or 180 coins
Top Bonus (27-coin version):	27,000 credits
Top Bonus (180-coin version):	180,000 credits
Progressive Reset:	$100,000
Average Hit Frequency:	33% (all lines active)
Long-term Payback Range:	88% to 89%

This MegaJackpots progressive is fitted with a top box mechanical wheel and a video screen that shows one of 43 clips from the actual movie during the bonus event. The bonus round is triggered by three bonus symbols on an active payline. At the end of the film clip, the player is prompted to press the spin button to begin rotating the big wheel which has multipliers of the line bet ranging from 25X to 1,000X.

RAWHIDE

Manufacturer:	Konami Gaming
Game Format:	Bonus video
Number of Reels:	5
Number of Paylines:	1-10, 1-20, 1-25, or 1-30
Denominations:	Penny, two cents, or nickel
Maximum Bet:	30 to 3,000 credits
Top Payout:	Line bet times 2,000 credits
Mystery Jackpot Thresholds (Mini):	$100
Mystery Jackpot Thresholds (Major):	$1,000
Average Hit Frequency:	77% (all lines active)
Long-term Payback Range:	85% to 96%

This Western-themed game has a two-level mystery progressive feature. The primary game is simple with plenty of wild symbols. Three or more bonus scatter symbols trigger up to 25 free spins and all jackpots are doubled. One or the other of the two progressive jackpots is awarded randomly, depending on how much is wagered.

RAZZ MA TAZZ

Manufacturer:	Aristocrat Technologies
Game Format:	Bonus video
Number of Reels:	5
Number of Paylines:	Scatter pay
Denominations:	Penny, two cents, or nickel
Maximum Bet:	200 or 500 credits
Top Payout (200-credit version):	240,000 credits
Top Payout (500-credit version):	600,000 credits
Average Hit Frequency:	75% (all reels active)
Long-term Payback Range:	88% to 97%

In this game, based on American jazz music, the player pays to activate reels instead of paylines, and the wins are based on scatter symbols. With all reels activated, every spin has 243 possible winning combinations. Triggering the secondary screen starts a special free-spin bonus round with up to 20 free spins and up to a 30X jackpot multiplier. The free spin bonus can be won again within the free bonus feature.

RED BARON

Manufacturer:	Aristocrat Technologies
Game Format:	Bonus video
Number of Reels:	5
Number of Paylines:	Scatter pay
Denominations:	Penny, two cents, or nickel
Maximum Bet:	200 or 500 credits
Top Payout (200-credit version):	240,000 credits
Top Payout (500-credit version):	600,000 credits
Average Hit Frequency:	75% (all reels active)
Long-term Payback Range:	88% to 97%

The theme of this game is based on the legendary German World War I fighter pilot. The player pays to activate reels instead of paylines, and the wins are based on scatter symbols. With all reels activated, every spin has 243 possible winning combinations. Triggering the secondary screen starts one of two special free-spin bonus rounds with up to 15 free spins and extra bonus credits.

RED HOTTIE

Manufacturer:	International Game Technology
Game Format:	Reel spinner, option-buy
Number of Reels:	3 or 4
Number of Paylines:	1
Denominations:	Quarter or dollar
Maximum Bet (3-reels):	2 coins
Maximum Bet (4-reels):	10 coins
Top Payout:	3,000 coins
Average Hit Frequency:	17%
Long-term Payback Range:	85% to 98%

In this game the player has the choice of betting two coins to activate three reels or betting ten coins to activate a fourth, which contains dice symbols. The winning rolls are four for a repeated roll, five for a mystery bonus, and six which starts the main bonus sequence. In this sequence, the player can win awards from five credits to 1,000 credits, which the player can accept or decline in the hope of getting a bigger amount.

RED, WHITE & BLUE (reel)

Manufacturer:	International Game Technology
Game Format:	Reel spinner, multiplier
Number of Reels:	3
Number of Paylines:	1
Denominations:	All or multidenominational
Maximum Bet:	1, 2, or 3 coins
Top Payout:	Set by casino
Average Hit Frequency:	16%
Long-term Payback Range:	85% to 98%

A classic three-reel, one-line multiplier that comes in one-, two-, and three-coin versions. This twenty-year-old game is still popular.

RED, WHITE & BLUE (video)

Manufacturer:	International Game Technology
Game Format:	Video, reel emulator
Number of Reels:	3
Number of Paylines:	1-9
Denominations:	All or multidenominational
Maximum Bet:	180 credits
Top Payout:	50,000 credits
Average Hit Frequency:	53% (all lines active)
Long-term Payback Range:	85% to 98%

Similar to the reel spinner version with a much higher hit frequency and the opportunity to bet a whole lot more money.

REEL 'EM IN: BIG BASS BUCKS

Manufacturer:	WMS Gaming
Game Format:	Bonus video
Number of Reels:	5
Number of Paylines:	1-9, 1-15, or 1-20
Denominations:	All denominations
Maximum Bet (9-line version):	9-180 credits
Maximum Bet (15-line version):	15-300 credits
Maximum Bet (20-line version):	20-400 credits
Top Payout:	50,000 credits (all versions)
Average Hit Frequency (9-line):	33% to 36% (all lines active)
Average Hit Frequency (15-line):	50% to 52% (all lines active)
Average Hit Frequency (20-line):	53% to 56% (all lines active)
Long-term Payback Range:	84% to 95%

This game is available to the casino in a large number of configurations involving the number of paylines, maximum bet, and denomination. Expect to find mostly penny, two cents, and nickel denominations. There are one primary and two secondary bonus features involving two (count 'em) screens, the top one showing the cartoon fishermen and the bottom one showing an underwater view of the fish.

RISING FIRE

Manufacturer:	Konami Gaming
Game Format:	Bonus video
Number of Reels:	5
Number of Paylines:	1-15, 1-20 or 1-25
Denominations:	All denominations from penny to $5
Maximum Bet:	5, 10, 20, or 50 credits per line
Top Payout:	Line bet times 20,000 credits
Average Hit Frequency:	40% (all lines active)
Long-term Payback Range:	88% to 96%

The main feature of this game with an Aztec temple theme, is the free-spin bonus. Three or more scattered temple symbols trigger 15 to 25 free spins. During the free spins, the Phoenix Rising From the Flames symbol is wild and multiplies the jackpot by 5X, 10X, or 20X. The bonus round can be retriggered during the free spins. Some versions of this game have the mystery progressive jackpot feature.

S&H GREEN STAMPS

Manufacturer:	Bally Technologies
Game Format:	Bonus video
Number of Reels:	5
Number of Paylines:	1-20
Denomination:	Penny
Maximum Bet:	1,000 credits
Top Payout:	Line bet times 6,000 credits
Average Hit Frequency:	50% (all lines active)
Long-term Payback Range:	86% to 96%

For those of us old enough to remember, this is a nostalgic throwback to the 1950s and 1960s when many people collected Green Stamps that they got with their purchases and pasted them into stamp books. The stamp books could then be exchanged for a variety of merchandise. In this game, the player collects stamp books and can exchange them for free spins and bonus credits.

SECRETS OF AFRICA

Manufacturer:	Atronic Americas
Game Format:	Bonus video
Number of Reels:	5
Number of Paylines:	1-9, 1-15, or 1-21
Denominations:	Penny, two cents, nickel, or quarter
Maximum Bet:	27 to 210 credits
Top Payout	
(9- and 15-line versions):	37,500 credits
Top Payout (21-line version):	125,000 credits
Average Hit Frequency (9-line):	29% (all lines active)
Average Hit Frequency (15-line):	31% (all lines active)
Average Hit Frequency (21-line):	36% (all lines active)
Long-term Payback Range:	86% to 94%

Two Golden Mask symbols pay a scatter award; three of them trigger the main free-spin bonus event, which initiates a round of ten to twelve free spins, along with a 2X jackpot multiplier. When certain symbols land on the first or fifth reel during the bonus event, additional free spins are added and the jackpot multiplier can increase to a maximum of 10X. Three versions of this game are available with different numbers of paylines and top awards.

SHOW ME THE MUMMY

Manufacturer:	Konami Gaming
Game Format:	Bonus video, progressive
Number of Reels:	5
Number of Paylines:	1-9
Denominations:	All denominations from penny to dollar
Maximum Bet:	9 to 900 credits, depending on denomination
Top Payout:	Progressive
Progressive Reset:	Casino dependent
Average Hit Frequency:	50% (all lines active)
Long-term Payback Range:	87% to 95%

The main character in this game is called Nigel, and lining up five Nigel symbols (assuming you made the maximum bet) wins the progressive jackpot. Three or more torch symbols on a payline starts the main bonus screen, which leads the player through a series of traps and tests that either continues to a higher bonus level or ends the bonus round. The unique bonus feature and the high hit frequency make this game fun to play.

THE SIGN OF ZODIAC

Manufacturer:	Atronic Americas
Game Format:	Bonus video
Number of Reels:	5
Number of Paylines:	1-5, 1-9, or 1-20
Denominations:	Penny, nickel, quarter, or dollar
Maximum Bet (5-line version):	5 or 25 credits
Maximum Bet (9-line version):	9, 45, or 90 credits
Maximum Bet (20-line version):	20, 100, or 200 credits
Top Payout:	25,000 credits
Average Hit Frequency:	40% to 50% (all lines active)
Long-term Payback Range:	88% to 98%

This is a standard video game that comes in several payline varieties, with a maximum bet as high as 200 credits in the 20-line version. There are two bonus features, which are started when three or more zodiac or horoscope symbols land on a payline. These bonus events may pay in credit awards, free spins, or, in one case, a Spin As Long As You Win sequence.

SIZZLING 7s

Manufacturer:	International Game Technology
Game Format:	Reel spinner, option-buy
Number of Reels:	3
Number of Paylines:	1
Denominations:	All or multidenominational
Maximum Bet:	3 coins
Top Payout:	1,000 coins
Average Hit Frequency:	13%
Long-term Payback Range:	85% to 98%

A three-reel option-buy game that comes only in a three-coin version. To qualify for the top award, you have to bet the three coins.

SPARKLING SEVENS

Manufacturer:	Konami Gaming
Game Format:	Reel spinner, option-buy
Number of Reels:	4
Number of Paylines:	1
Denominations:	Nickel, quarter, half, dollar, $2, or $5
Maximum Bet:	3 coins
Top Payout:	10,000 coins
Average Hit Frequency:	16%
Long-term Payback Range:	87% to 98%

This is actually a three-reel machine where the fourth reel displays bonus features that apply to winning combinations. The bonus reel contains 2X, 5X, and 10X multipliers, a respin, and a mystery bonus. The top jackpot is won when three pink 7s land on the payline and there is a 10X symbol on the screen. Of course, since this is an option-buy (buy-a-pay) game, the bonus reel is only active for a maximum wager.

STAR DRIFTER

Manufacturer:	Aristocrat Technologies
Game Format:	Bonus video
Number of Reels:	5
Number of Paylines:	2-50
Denominations:	Penny, two cents, or nickel
Maximum Bet:	1,000 credits
Top Payout:	Line bet times 20,000 credits
Average Hit Frequency:	70% (all lines active)
Long-term Payback Range:	88% to 97%

This video game with a Wild West theme has a five-by-four grid with four rows of symbols on the five reels. Although the game has 50 paylines, each credit buys two paylines. Three playing card symbols scattered anywhere on the reels starts the bonus round with an initial ten free spins. With each free spin, a wild symbol is added, which ultimately drives up the hit frequency to an incredible 70%. More free spins are added if the scatter symbols appear again.

STAR TREK

Manufacturer:	WMS Gaming
Game Format:	Bonus video
Number of Reels:	5
Number of Paylines:	1-25
Denominations:	All denominations from penny to $50
Maximum Bet:	1,050 credits
Top Payout:	300,000 credits
Average Hit Frequency:	41% (all lines active)
Long-term Payback Range:	87% to 94%

This game carries the theme and images of the original Star Trek television series in the form of sensory immersion technology and surround sound. Furthermore, a central server permits the slot experience to be continuous over several sessions by using a log-in code that is printed on the ticket and can be used to resume the game where it was left off. The game itself has several episodes, and each episode has several bonus features, in addition to a bonus triggered by game symbols, which gives the player a choice between a free-spin bonus and a pick-a-tile bonus game.

STAR WARS: A NEW HOPE

Manufacturer:	International Game Technology
Game Format:	Bonus video or progressive
Number of Reels:	5
Number of Paylines:	1-30
Denomination:	Penny
Maximum Bet:	300 credits
Top Payout (non-progressive ver.):	$25,000
Reset (multisite progressive):	$1 million in Nevada
Reset (multisite progressive):	$500,000 elsewhere
Average Hit Frequency:	50% (all lines active)
Long-term Payback Range:	88% to 91%

To distinguish this Star Wars version, the top of the cabinet has a large replica of the Death Star planet-killing weapon. The theme is fully realized in this phenomenal game, which is actually three games in one. There are three different sets of reel symbols, animation, and sound that are activated depending on how much is wagered. A multitude of bonus events brings the experience of the original film to life. With a wager of maximum coins, lining up five Star Wars symbols on the first payline wins the progressive jackpot, which resets at $1 million in Nevada. The game comes in a non-progressive as well as a MegaJackpots multisite progressive version.

STAR WARS: THE EMPIRE STRIKES BACK

Manufacturer:	International Game Technology
Game Format:	Bonus video or progressive
Number of Reels:	5
Number of Paylines:	1-30
Denomination:	Penny
Maximum Bet:	300 credits
Top Payout	
(non-progressive version):	Varies with jurisdiction
Reset (multisite progressive):	$5 million in Nevada
Reset (multisite progressive):	Varies elsewhere
Average Hit Frequency:	40% (all lines active)
Long-term Payback Range:	87% to 94%

In this Star Wars version, a sculpture of Yoda looks down from the top of the machine, standing above a new variation of the bonus wheel. Several different bonus events result in the accumulation of credits, credit multipliers, and free spins. One free spin event can go as long as 100 spins, and continues until both a Han Solo and Boba Fett symbol land on the reels. If the Han Solo symbol lands first, that entire reel becomes wild and remains wild for the remaining free spins. In another, the top box wheel rotates to the side and spins three times to show a number of extra free spins. The game comes in a non-progressive as well as a MegaJackpots multisite progressive version.

SWEET LIBERTY DELUXE

Manufacturer:	Aristocrat Technologies
Game Format:	Bonus video
Number of Reels:	5
Number of Paylines:	1-9 or 1-20
Denominations:	All denominations from penny to dollar
Maximum Bet (9-line version):	45, 90, or 180 credits
Maximum Bet (20-line version):	100, 200, 500, or 1,000 credits
Top Payout (45 or 100 credits):	15,000 credits
Top Payout (90 or 200 credits):	30,000 credits
Top Payout (180 credits):	60,000 credits
Top Payout (500 credits):	75,000 credits
Top Payout (1,000 credits):	150,000 credits
Average Hit Frequency(9-line):	33% (all lines active)
Average Hit Frequency(20-line):	45% (all lines active)
Long-term Payback Range:	88% to 97%

In this patriotic-themed game, the Statue of Liberty symbol anywhere on reels one and five triggers ten free spins. During the free spins, a coin symbol showing up anywhere awards up to 100 credits times the amount of the wager. The dollar sign symbol is wild for everything except scatter pays. When three or more coin symbols appear anywhere on the reels, the award is 100 times the amount wagered.

TABBY CASH

Manufacturer:	Atronic Americas
Game Format:	Bonus video
Number of Reels:	5
Number of Paylines:	1-9 or 1-21
Denominations:	Penny, two cents, or nickel
Maximum Bet:	27, 90, 210, or 525 credits
Top Payout (9-line, 27-credit version):	30,000 credits
Top Payout (9-line, 90-credit version):	100,000 credits
Top Payout (21-line, 210-credit version):	100,000 credits
Top Payout (21-line, 525-credit version):	250,000 credits
Average Hit Frequency (9-line):	28% (all lines active)
Average Hit Frequency (21-line):	32% (all lines active)
Long-term Payback Range:	86% to 94%

Male and female cat characters populate the feline theme of this game. Three scatter symbols start the main bonus sequence that awards the player with nine free spins to start the Spin As Long As You Win feature. During the free spins, the paylines disappear and all wins are paid as scatters. The free spins then continue as long as the player gets at least one winning combination, or until the player runs out of cat lives.

TEMPLE OF TREASURE

Manufacturer:	International Game Technology
Game Format:	Bonus reel, option buy, progressive
Number of Reels:	3 or 5
Number of Paylines (3-reel):	1
Number of Paylines (5-reel):	1-25
Denomination:	All denominations from penny to dollar
Maximum Bet (3-reel):	3 coins
Maximum Bet (5-reel):	125 coins
Top Payout:	Progressive
Progressive Reset:	$100,000
Average Hit Frequency (3-reel):	17%
Average Hit Frequency (5-reel):	63% (all lines active)
Long-term Payback:	86% to 93%

This progressive has a three-reel, one-line format and a five-reel, 25-line format. They are both option-buy (buy-a-pay) games, so you have to wager the maximum to get a chance at the progressive award, as well as the bonus round. When the bonus is triggered, the top box activates, and this leads to a bonus award or to the multisite progressive jackpot. At the top of the game board in the top box are three emerald symbols. Landing on all three wins the progressive.

TEN TIMES PAY

Manufacturer:	International Game Technology
Game Format:	Reel spinner, modified multiplier
Number of Reels:	3
Number of Paylines:	1
Denominations:	All or multidenominational
Maximum Bet:	2 or 3 coins
Top Payout:	Up to 25,000 coins
Average Hit Frequency:	13%
Long-term Payback:	85%

A three-reel modified multiplier that has 10X substitute multiplier symbols to add a little excitement.

TEXAS TEA

Manufacturer:	International Game Technology
Game Format:	Bonus video
Number of Reels:	5
Number of Paylines:	1-9
Denominations:	All
Maximum Bet:	180 credits
Top Payout:	200,000 credits
Average Hit Frequency:	44% (all lines active)
Long-term Payback Range:	85% to 98%

This game, with the comical oil tycoon character, Texas Ted, has been around for a while without losing popularity. Three Texas Ted scatter symbols gets the player an oil dividend check that pays credit awards. The main bonus screen prompts the player to place oil derricks in various parts of Texas. The oil pumps go to work, and the more oil they pump, the more credits are won. It's a simple, but fun game to play, especially with the decent hit frequency.

THREE WITCHES

Manufacturer:	Atronic Americas
Game Format:	Bonus video
Number of Reels:	5
Number of Paylines:	1-9 or 1-21
Denominations:	All denominations
Maximum Bet:	27, 90, 210, or 525 credits
Top Payout (9-line, 27-credit version):	15,000 credits
Top Payout (9-line, 90-credit version):	30,000 credits
Top Payout (21-line, 210-credit version):	100,000 credits
Top Payout (21-line, 525-credit version):	250,000 credits
Average Hit Frequency (9-line):	37% (all lines active)
Average Hit Frequency (21-line):	46% (all lines active)
Long-term Payback Range:	86% to 94%

The three witches are triggers for the free-spin bonus round when they appear anywhere on the first, third, and fifth reels. Along with the wizard, they become wild symbols during the ten free-spin sequence. With four wild symbols it's very likely that the free spin event is retriggered. Of the many versions of this game, the 21-line penny version is probably the best because of the high hit frequency.

TIME FOR MONEY

Manufacturer:	Atronic Americas
Game Format:	Bonus video
Number of Reels:	5
Number of Paylines:	1-9, 1-15, or 1-21
Denominations:	All denominations
Maximum Bet:	90, 150, or 210 credits
Top Payout (9- and 15-line versions):	37,500 credits
Top Payout (21-line version):	125,000 credits
Average Hit Frequency (9-line):	50% (all lines active)
Average Hit Frequency (15-line):	51% (all lines active)
Average Hit Frequency (21-line):	60% (all lines active)
Long-term Payback Range:	86% to 94%

Time travel is the theme for this slot game, which has two main bonus events. When the bonus is triggered, the player has a choice of taking the credits offered or spinning the reels to try for a larger amount. In the other bonus event, the symbols on some reels turn into credit amounts, and the player selects one reel to spin for a credit bonus. This game also has the Spin-As-Long-As-You-Win feature.

TOP DOLLAR (reel)

Manufacturer:	International Game Technology
Game Format:	Reel spinner, option-buy
Number of Reels:	3
Number of Paylines:	1
Denominations:	All or multidenominational
Maximum Bet:	2 or 3 coins
Top Payout:	2,500 or 4,000 coins
Average Hit Frequency:	14%
Long-term Payback Range:	85% to 98%

A three-reel option-buy game that comes in a two- or three-coin version. To qualify for the top box bonus of up to 1,000 credits, you have to bet the maximum.

TOP DOLLAR (video)

Manufacturer:	International Game Technology
Game Format:	Bonus video
Number of Reels:	5
Number of Paylines:	1-20
Denomination:	Penny
Maximum Bet:	1,000 credits
Top Payout:	250,000 credits ($2,500)
Average Hit Frequency:	60% (all lines active)
Long-term Payback:	85% to 94%

This is the video version of the Top Dollar reel spinner. Three or more Top Dollar symbols on a payline starts the Top Dollar bonus, where lights flash behind stacks of cash. When the flashing stops and one or more stacks are illuminated, the player has the option of accepting the amount shown or trying again, hoping to get a bigger bonus. The player can do this up to four times, but must take the last one. The bonus is multiplied by the line bet to arrive at the final award.

TOP GUN

Manufacturer:	WMS Gaming
Game Format:	Bonus video or progressive
Number of Reels:	5
Number of Paylines:	1-15, 1-20, or 1-25
Denominations:	Penny or nickel
Maximum Bet:	60 to 200 credits
Top Payout (non-progressive):	10,000 credits
Progressive Reset (multisite):	$500,000
Average Hit Frequency:	42% to 45% (all lines active)
Long-term Payback Range:	88% to 92%

This game creates a completely new slot experience in the form of sensory immersion technology. The surround sound and vibrating seat make you feel that you're in the cockpit of a fighter jet. It may seem like a realistic video game, but it's actually a very solidly-designed slot game, and the various bonus events are where most of the sensory immersion comes into play. Aside from their entertainment value, the bonus sequences provide many different ways to accumulate credits. Where progressive jackpots are not permitted, the game is offered in a stand-alone version.

TREASURE CHESS

Manufacturer:	Aristocrat Technologies
Game Format:	Bonus video
Number of Reels:	5
Number of Paylines:	1-9 or 1-20
Denominations:	All denominations from penny to dollar
Maximum Bet (9-line version):	45, 90, or 180 credits
Maximum Bet (20-line version):	100, 200, 500, or 1,000 credits
Top Payout (9-line):	50,000 credits
Top Payout (20-line):	100,000 credits
Average Hit Frequency (9-line):	50% (all lines active)
Average Hit Frequency (20-line):	58% (all lines active)
Long-term Payback Range:	88% to 97%

Of particular interest to chess players, this is a video game based on a chess theme in which the player "purchases" the chess pieces in each activated payline. These pieces then capture all the identical chess pieces using standard chess moves, resulting in credit awards. The machine does this automatically, but if you have the slightest understanding of chess, you will soon comprehend what is happening.

TREASURES OF TROY

Manufacturer:	International Game Technology
Game Format:	Bonus video
Number of Reels:	5
Number of Paylines:	1-40
Denominations:	Penny
Maximum Bet:	4,000 credits
Top Payout:	200,000 credits
Average Hit Frequency:	26% (all lines active)
Long-term Payback Range:	90% to 98%

Wagering at least one credit for each of the 40 paylines, plus another equal bet, enables the multiway option in which each of the 20 symbols acts as its own independent reel. Thus, all the payline wins plus all the scatter pays combine for a total of 1024 possible ways to win on every spin. Even though this is a penny game, you can wager up to 100 credits per line for an unbelievable total of $40 per spin.

TRIPLE DIAMOND

Manufacturer:	International Game Technology
Game Format:	Reel spinner, multiplier
Number of Reels:	3
Number of Paylines:	1
Denominations:	All or multidenominational
Maximum Bet:	1, 2, or 3 coins
Top Payout:	Up to 4,000 coins
Average Hit Frequency:	14%
Long-term Payback Range:	85% to 98%

A three-reel multiplier that comes in one-, two-, and three-coin versions. The Triple Diamond symbols are wild multipliers. One of them on a payline multiplies any jackpot by 3X, two of them multiply any jackpot by 9X.

TRIPLE DOUBLE DIAMOND

Manufacturer:	International Game Technology
Game Format:	Reel spinner, multiplier
Number of Reels:	3
Number of Paylines:	1
Denominations:	All or multidenominational
Maximum Bet:	2 or 3 coins
Top Payout:	Up to 4,000 coins
Average Hit Frequency:	12%
Long-term Payback Range:	85% to 98%

A three-reel multiplier that comes in two- and three-coin versions, and includes wild multiplier symbols.

VILLAGE PEOPLE PARTY

Manufacturer:	WMS Gaming
Game Format:	Bonus video
Number of Reels:	5
Number of Paylines:	1-9, 1-20, or 1-25
Denominations:	All denominations from penny to dollar
Maximum Bet (9-line version):	270 credits
Maximum Bet (20-line version):	600 credits
Maximum Bet (25-line version):	750 credits
Top Payout (credits):	Line bet times 5,000 credits
Average Hit Frequency (9-line):	35% (all lines active)
Average Hit Frequency (20-line):	48% (all lines active)
Average Hit Frequency (25-line):	56% (all lines active)
Long-term Payback Range:	87% to 94%

The scene is New York's Greenwich Village with a bunch of comic characters. The characters come alive in the bonus event where the screen displays six Village People. The player is prompted to select one of them to win credits that are multiples of the total bet. A selection of records appears, from which the player picks to get more credit awards and a bonus multiplier. When the Party Pooper shows up, the bonus sequence ends.

WHEEL OF FORTUNE (reel)

Manufacturer:	International Game Technology
Game Format:	Reel spinner, progressive
Number of Reels:	3
Number of Paylines:	1
Denominations:	Quarter, half, or dollar
Maximum Bet:	3 coins
Top Payout:	Progressive
Progressive Reset (quarter version):	$200,000
Progressive Reset (half dollar version):	$500,000
Progressive Reset (dollar version):	$1 million
Average Hit Frequency:	12%
Long-term Payback Range:	84% to 89%

Wheel of Fortune is the most popular progressive slot machine theme of all time, with its spinning-wheel top box always attracting attention. This three-reel MegaJackpots machine comes in quarter, half dollar, and dollar versions, and in each case, you have to wager three coins to qualify for the progressive award. There is also a two-coin $5.00 version with a reset that starts at $1 million.

WHEEL OF FORTUNE (video)

Manufacturer:	International Game Technology
Game Format:	Bonus video, progressive
Number of Reels:	5
Number of Paylines:	1-5 or 1-30
Denomination (5-line version):	Nickel
Denomination (30-line version):	Penny
Maximum Bet:	400 credits
Top Progressive Reset:	$1.5 million in Nevada
Top Progressive Reset:	Elsewhere varies by jurisdiction
Other Reset (red):	$500
Other Reset (green):	$75
Other Reset (blue):	$25
Other Reset (purple):	$10
Average Hit Frequency:	50% (all lines active)
Long-term Payback Range:	88% to 94%

The video version of this theme is usually found in the penny denomination, and has five multilevel progressive jackpots. The top progressive is won by lining up five Wheel of Fortune symbols on the first payline with a maximum wager. On the penny machine, the player must bet 30¢ to activate all the paylines, plus an additional 20¢, to light up one of the pointers around the wheel. Every additional 50¢ lights another bonus arrow, and $4 lights all eight. With all eight arrows activated during a bonus round, the player is guaranteed to win one progressive award, and possibly two.

WHERE'S THE GOLD

Manufacturer:	Aristocrat Technologies
Game Format:	Bonus video
Number of Reels:	5
Number of Paylines:	1-25
Denominations:	All denominations from penny to dollar
Maximum Bet:	250, 500, 1,000, or 1,250 credits
Top Payout (250-credit version):	10,000 credits
Top Payout (500-credit version):	20,000 credits
Top Payout (1,000-credit version):	40,000 credits
Top Payout (1,250-credit version):	50,000 credits
Average Hit Frequency:	50% (all lines active)
Long-term Payback Range:	88% to 95%

This standard 25-line video slot comes in four versions with top jackpots of 10,000 to 50,000 credits. The theme is gold prospecting, and three or more dynamite scatter-pay symbols in the primary game initiate a bonus screen depicting cartoon mining characters. Selecting one of the characters results in being awarded three to ten free spins.

WILD COUGAR

Manufacturer:	Aristocrat Technologies
Game Format:	Bonus video
Number of Reels:	5
Number of Paylines:	1-5 or 1-9
Denominations:	All denominations from penny to dollar
Maximum Bet (5-line version):	50 credits
Maximum Bet (9-line version):	90 credits
Top Payout:	50,000 credits
Average Hit Frequency (5-line):	23% (all lines active)
Average Hit Frequency (9-line):	30% (all lines active)
Long-term Payback Range:	88% to 97%

This is a standard video game that comes in five- and nine-line versions. The Wild Cougar substitute symbol, which occurs frequently, also includes scatter pays. In addition, there is a double-or-nothing proposition after every winning combination.

WILD FANGS

Manufacturer:	Atronic Americas
Game Format:	Bonus video
Number of Reels:	5
Number of Paylines:	1-9 or 1-25
Denominations:	Penny, two cents, or nickel
Maximum Bet:	27, 90, 250, or 625 credits
Top Payout (9-line, 27-credit version):	37,500 credits
Top Payout (9-line, 90-credit version):	125,000 credits
Top Payout (25-line, 250-credit version):	125,000 credits
Top Payout (25-line, 625-credit version):	312,500 credits
Average Hit Frequency (9-line):	21% (all lines active)
Average Hit Frequency (25-line):	25% (all lines active)
Long-term Payback Range:	86% to 96%

In the 9-line version, three or more WolfMoon symbols start a free-spin round. The player gets 15 free spins and all wins are tripled, and if a wild wolf symbol is part of another free-spin combination, the tripled wins are doubled. In the 25-line version, three, four, or five WolfMoon symbols get the player 15, 20, or 25 free spins, respectively. These wins are doubled, and the appearance of the wild wolf symbol multiplies the wins five more times. In both versions, re-triggers can accumulate up to 300 free spins.

WILD PANDA

Manufacturer:	Aristocrat Technologies
Game Format:	Bonus video
Number of Reels:	5
Number of Paylines:	1-100
Denominations:	Penny, two cents, or nickel
Maximum Bet:	1,000 credits
Top Payout:	40,000 credits
Average Hit Frequency:	40% (all lines active)
Long-term Payback Range:	88% to 95%

With 100 paylines, it's almost impossible to identify all of them (some go in a circle), however, the game will show them when you win. When the letters P-A-N-D-A are spelled out across the five reels, five free spins are awarded and all the PANDA letters become wild, increasing your chances of getting more free spins. Three or more Wild Panda symbols during the free spins pay up to 4,000 credits times the line bet.

WILD ROSE (line game)

Manufacturer:	Bally Technologies
Game Format:	Reel spinner, line game
Number of Reels:	3
Number of Paylines:	3 or 5
Denominations:	Nickel, quarter, or dollar
Maximum Bet:	3 or 5 coins
Top Payout (3-line version):	2400 coins
Top Payout (5-line version):	5,000 coins
Average Hit Frequency:	13% (all lines active)
Long-term Payback Range:	84% to 96%

A classic three-reel line game that comes in three- and five-payline versions, and has multiplying wild symbols. Don't confuse this with the multiplier version (below), which has only one payline.

WILD ROSE (multiplier)

Manufacturer:	Bally Technologies
Game Format:	Reel spinner, true multiplier
Number of Reels:	3
Number of Paylines:	1
Denominations:	Nickel, quarter, or dollar
Maximum Bet:	2 or 3 coins
Top Payout (2-coin version):	1600 coins
Top Payout (3-coin version):	2400 coins
Average Hit Frequency:	13%
Long-term Payback Range:	86% to 97%

A classic three-reel true multiplier that comes in two- and three-coin versions, and has multiplying wild symbols. A very good game for novice reel spinners.

WILD WOLF

Manufacturer:	International Game Technology
Game Format:	Bonus video
Number of Reels:	5
Number of Paylines:	1-50
Denomination:	Penny
Maximum Bet:	500 credits
Top Payout:	10,000 credits
Average Hit Frequency:	35% (all lines active)
Long-term Payback Range:	86% to 98%

This is a modified version of Wolf Run (below) in a 50-line format. Multiple wild symbols tend to land in a cluster, resulting in multiple wins on different paylines. The wild symbols will often dominate the screen, covering two or more complete rows and creating dozens of paying combinations. A free-spin bonus round takes advantage of the wild symbols, producing more wins and more spins.

WOLF RUN

Manufacturer:	International Game Technology
Game Format:	Bonus video
Number of Reels:	5
Number of Paylines:	1-40
Denomination:	Penny
Maximum Bet:	400, 800, or 2,000 credits
Top Payout:	Line bet times 1,000 credits
Average Hit Frequency:	25% (all lines active)
Long-term Payback Range:	87% to 98%

The reels in the game have a four-by-five configuration with oversized symbols. When bonus wolf symbols appear on the three middle reels in any position, the free-spin feature is triggered and the player is awarded five free spins. If the bonus symbols land again during a free spin, another five is awarded. This can go on for a maximum of 255 free spins. Wild symbols also add to the accumulation of credits.

WORLD POKER TOUR

Manufacturer:	International Game Technology
Game Format:	Bonus video, progressive
Number of Reels:	5
Number of Paylines:	1-20
Denomination:	Penny
Maximum Bet:	300 credits
Top Payout:	Progressive
Progressive Reset:	$1 million
Average Hit Frequency:	35% (all lines active)
Long-term Payback:	88%

This poker game, with the theme and images of the World Poker Tour, is in the form of a MegaJackpots multisite progressive. The progressive jackpot is won with a hand of five aces. To qualify for the free-spin bonus round, the player must cover all 20 paylines and make an additional ante wager of ten credits. At every spin, a seven-card poker hand appears above the reels. This hand triggers the bonus if it is a full house or better.

YOUNG FRANKENSTEIN

Manufacturer:	International Game Technology
Game Format:	Bonus video, progressive
Number of Reels:	5
Number of Paylines:	1-9 or 1-15
Denomination:	Nickel
Maximum Bet (9-line version):	45 credits
Maximum Bet (15-line version):	75 credits
Top Payout:	Progressive
Progressive Reset:	$100,000
Average Hit Frequency:	50% (all lines active)
Long-term Payback Range:	88% to 89%

This is a MegaJackpots multisite progressive that is based on the Mel Brooks movie, with a large top box that replicates Dr. Frankenstein's laboratory. All the principal characters are featured with sound bites and animation from the movie. In one of the two bonus events, the player gets to select a brain, with a corresponding award. The reset is $100,000 and the progressive jackpot is paid in a lump sum, but to win it you have to wager the maximum amount.

ZULU DAWN

Manufacturer:	Konami Gaming
Game Format:	Bonus video
Number of Reels:	5
Number of Paylines:	Scatter
Denominations:	All denominations from penny to $5
Maximum Bet:	1,500 coins
Top Payout:	Bet times 2,000 coins
Average Hit Frequency:	43% (all reels active)
Long-term Payback Range:	82% to 96%

This five-reel game with an African warrior theme, is a little unconventional even for a scatter-pay video. The second and fourth reels have four symbols each, while the other reels have three. All wins are paid as scatters or combinations on adjacent reels, left-to-right, making a total of 432 possible wins on every spin. There are two bonus events. One of them plays out on a second screen, and the other is a free-spin round.

GLOSSARY

Ace

The highest-ranking card in video poker. May also be used as the lowest card in an A-2-3-4-5 straight or straight flush.

Ace kicker

A lone ace that is held (usually with a pair), when drawing replacement cards. Not a recommended strategy in video poker.

Action

The total amount of money bet. Win or lose, the same dollar bet fifty times, constitutes $50 worth of action.

Banking game

A slot machine in which points or some form of assets are accumulated in a "bank" and eventually paid out as credits.

Bankroll

The amount of money a person designates for gambling.

Bar

A common symbol on slot machine reels.

BET MAX button

Pressing this button causes two actions to occur. First, it registers a maximum credit bet, whatever it might be for that machine. If it is a two-coin machine it will register two coins, if it is a three-coin machine it will register three coins, and so forth. Second, it automatically spins the reels; you don't have to press the SPIN button. On some machines, this button is marked PLAY MAX CREDITS.

BET ONE button

Pressing this button will register in the machine as a one-credit bet. It is exactly the same as if you put one coin into the slot, which is an alternative. If you press the button a second time, it will register as a two-credit bet, and so forth. On some machines, this button is marked BET 1 CREDIT.

Big Bertha

A giant slot machine with eight to ten reels, often placed near the entrance of a casino to lure potential slot players. Not a good machine to play.

Blank

A stop on a slot machine reel with no symbols. A few machines give a minimum payout for three blanks.

Bonus game

A slot machine in which certain symbol combinations cause a bonus mode to appear on a secondary screen.

Buy-a-pay game

Another term for an option-buy game.

Cage

Short for cashier's cage, where casino chips may be exchanged for cash and other financial transactions may be consummated.

Candle

The light on top of a slot cabinet that indicates the machine denomination and signals for an attendant when you press the CHANGE button.

Carousel

A group of slot machines arranged in a circle or an oval, which is often surrounding an elevated change booth.

CASH OUT button

Pressing this button converts any credits accumulated in the machine to coins or a cash ticket. This button is sometimes marked CASH/CREDIT or COLLECT.

GLOSSARY

Cash ticket

A printed paper coupon that can be redeemed for cash or inserted in another ticket-equipped game machine.

Casino advantage

The mathematical edge a casino has over the player, which is usually stated as a percentage.

Casino host

The casino employee who caters to the needs of high-stakes players.

Casino manager

The head honcho for all gaming operations.

Catch

Each number on a keno machine that matches one of the drawn numbers.

Change booth

A booth set up to convert a player's currency to coins or coins to currency. Change booths used to be a common feature in most casino areas.

CHANGE button

Pressing this button summons the change person. You should also press the button whenever something seems to go wrong with the machine. This button is often marked SERVICE.

Change person

The casino employee who used to roam the slot machine area and make change for the players.

Chasing losses

Raising the betting level in an attempt to recoup losses. Not a recommended procedure.

Cherry

A common symbol on slot machine reels.

Cold machine

A slot machine that is paying less than its expected payback.

Comp

Shortened term for the complimentary rewards—such as rooms, meals, or show tickets—given to big players.

Credits

Instead of paying out coins, most modern slot machines keep track of winnings in the form of credits that can be converted to coins or a cash ticket by pressing the CASH OUT button. The accumulated credits can also be played.

DEAL button

A button on a video poker machine that directs it to deal the next hand.

DEAL–DRAW button

A button on a video poker machine that combines the functions of a deal button and a draw button.

Denomination

The minimum coin or credit value required to play a slot machine. The most popular denominations are penny, nickel and quarter.

Deuces wild

All four deuces in the deck are designated as wild cards. See Wild card.

Discard

A card that is not held when drawing replacement cards.

Draw

The action in draw poker or video poker during which cards are drawn from the deck to replace those that have been discarded by the players. In blackjack and baccarat, adding cards to a hand.

DRAW button

A button on a video poker machine that directs it to draw replacements for all the cards that were not held.

Draw poker

A game of closed poker in which there is a one-time opportunity to replace unwanted cards in the player's hand with new cards drawn from the deck.

Edge

A statistical advantage. Usually the casino's advantage.

Even money

A bet that, if won, pays one-to-one odds.

Five-of-a-kind

Five cards, all of the same rank. Since a standard deck has only four cards of each rank (one in each suit), this must include a designated wild card such as a deuce or a joker.

Flush

Five cards of the same suit.

Four straight

Four of the five cards needed for a straight.

Four-card royal

Four of the five cards needed for a royal flush.

Four-flush

Four of the five cards needed for a flush; four cards of the same suit.

Four-of-a-kind

Four cards of the same rank.

Full house

Three-of-a-kind and a pair.

Garbage hand

A hand of no potential value that does not even contain a low pair.

Glass

The posted chart on a slot machine showing the winning symbol combinations and the payouts.

Handpay

A jackpot payoff or a cashout that is made by an attendant rather than by the machine.

High roller

A gambler who plays for high stakes.

Hit frequency

The number of wins as a percentage of the total number of spins on a slot machine. For example, a 20 percent hit frequency would be an average of one win for every five spins.

HOLD button

One of five buttons on a video poker machine that designates a card to be held (not discarded) when the draw occurs. Also, HOLD-CANCEL

Hopper

The container inside a slot machine that holds the coins used to pay off wins or a cashout.

Hot machine

A slot machine that is paying more than its expected payback.

House

The casino, the bank, or the game operator.

House edge

The difference between the actual odds and the payoff odds, usually stated as a percentage, which is the mathematical edge the house has over the player. Also called casino advantage, house advantage, house percentage, or P.C.

House percentage

The difference between the amount of money taken in by a machine and the amount paid out over the long term. This difference is the casino profit.

Jackpot

The largest payout on any particular machine. Also, any big win with a large payout.

Jacks or better

A game in which a pair of jacks is the lowest-paying hand.

Joker

An extra card in the deck that is designated as a wild card. See Wild card.

Kicker

An unmatched card held in the hand when drawing replacement cards. Not a recommended strategy in video poker.

Lemon

A common symbol on slot machine reels.

Line

Short for payline.

Line game

Another term for a multiple payline game.

Local progressive

Similar progressive machines, usually in a bank or carousel, which are linked together within a single casino.

Loose machine

A slot machine programmed for a higher than average long-term payback.

Loss limit

An arbitrary point in the value of your playing stake or your winnings, below which you stop playing. You set this value, which may be an absolute amount or a percentage of winnings, to protect your stake or your profits.

Low pair

In video poker, any pair that does not pay. In jacks-or-better, low pairs are 2 through 10. In table poker, a pair too small to open the betting.

Maximum bet

The largest number of coins or credits that can be wagered on one spin of a slot machine.

Multi-Game machine

A slot machine in which the player has a choice of several different games, usually including video poker.

Multiple payline game

A slot machine that has more than one payline. Wagering more coins or credits can activate the additional paylines.

Multiplier game
A slot machine in which the number of coins or credits wagered multiplies the amount of the payout.

Odds
The mathematical ratio of the number of ways to win versus the number of ways to lose.

One-armed bandit
An old slang term used for slot machines, indicating that the payouts were very poor.

Option-buy game
A slot machine in which additional winning symbol combinations are activated by betting the maximum number of coins or credits. Also called a buy-a-pay game.

Pair
Two cards of the same rank.

Payback
The total long-term winnings as a percent of the total amount bet.

Payline
A line across the window in front of the reels that shows where a winning symbol combination has to be aligned for a payoff. Some games have several paylines.

Payoff
The amount paid for a winning symbol combination.

Payout
Another term for payoff.

Paytable
A chart, usually above the reels, showing the winning symbol combinations and the payout amounts. On a video machine, the paytable may be displayed on the screen by pressing the PAYTABLE button.

PAYTABLE button
Pressing this button on a video game brings the paytable to the screen. Often, it is several pages in length. Sometimes this button is marked SEE PAYS.

Progressive jackpot

A dynamic top jackpot that grows larger by pooling a fraction of each wager as the games are played. Groups of machines are usually linked together, all contributing to the same progressive jackpot.

Random number generator (RNG)

The RNG is one of the chips on the internal computer board of a slot machine. It generates thousands of random numbers a second, and each random number sequence defines a specific set of reel positions or symbols.

Reel

Side-by-side rotating wheels displaying various symbols on the outside rims. A small section of the reels may be viewed through a window, which usually exposes about three rows of symbols.

Scatter symbols

Symbols that result in a payoff when they appear anywhere in the reel window.

Secondary screen

A bonus screen that is initiated by certain symbol combinations.

Sequential royal flush

A royal flush in which the five cards are displayed on the video poker screen in rank sequence as: 10-J-Q-K-A or A-K-Q-J-10, depending on how the particular machine defines it.

Shift boss

The top manager during the course of a single work shift.

Slot floor

The area of a casino designated for slot machines.

Slot manager

The top manager for the slot department of the casino.

Slot mechanic

The casino employee who is responsible for maintaining the proper mechanical and electronic operation of the slot machines.

SPIN button

After indicating the number of credits or inserting one or more coins, pressing this button starts the game by causing the reels to spin. On some machines, this button is marked SPIN REELS.

Spinning reel machine

A slot machine with actual mechanical spinning reels, although the reels are now computer controlled.

Spot

A marked number on a keno machine.

Stake

Another term for bankroll.

Stand-alone progressive

A solitary progressive slot machine that is not linked to any other machine.

STAND button

A button on a video poker machine that automatically puts a hold on all five cards.

Stop

The position of a reel when it comes to rest. A reel may stop when a symbol is under the payline or when the blank space between two symbols falls under the payline.

Straight

Five cards of consecutive rank, with mixed suits.

Straight flush

Five cards of consecutive rank, all of the same suit.

Substitute symbol

Another term for wild symbol.

Suit

The name of one of the four families of thirteen cards that make up a standard deck. The four suits are spades, hearts, clubs, and diamonds.

Symbols

The pictures of various objects that appear on the slot machine reels.

GLOSSARY

Three-of-a-kind
> Three cards of the same rank.

Tight machine
> A slot machine programmed for a lower than average long-term payback.

Top box
> An illuminated case above the reels or video screen that displays the game theme and/or additional bonus features.

Top payout
> The maximum amount that can be won on a slot machine by a single spin.

Touchscreen
> A video screen where you can touch an object to select it.

Two pair
> Two cards of the same rank and two cards of another rank.

Video keno
> A keno game that is played on a special slot machine instead of with paper tickets.

Video machine
> A slot machine in which the spinning reels are simulated on a video screen. Also called a video game.

Video poker
> A form of draw poker that is played on a special slot machine instead of with playing cards.

Wide Area Progressive Slot (WAPS)
> One of a large number of similar progressive machines that are linked together over a wide geographic area such as a city or a state.

Wild symbol
> A symbol that can substitute for any other symbol on the reels, often called substitute symbols. Wild symbols can combine with other symbols to produce a winning combination.

Window
> The glass area in front of the reels where the payline and the symbols are viewed.

FIVE BALL LOTTO WHEELS

Prof. Jones' Strategy for Non-Computer Users

SPECIAL 5-BALL STRATEGY PACKAGE These are the **master strategy** five ball wheels that allow you to play your **best numbers** and go for the big wins that other players dream about! **Popular and powerful**, these wheels get you ready for the action.

30 WHEELS INCLUDED A **wide variety of wheels** covers all situations, from **5 game plays** with a variety of best numbers, to **24 game wheels**, to even others covering more than 20 best number picks. You'll find wheels such as 7 numbers/12 plays (7/12), 11/3, 19/18, 6/6 and 25 more great wheeling combinations.

OTHER FEATURES You also receive 20 5-Ball Lotto Sum Templates, a clear template for ease-of-use in wheeling best numbers, a 5-Ball Lotto Sum chart to provide a number range, and a guide to number-choosing strategies to help you win.

BONUS Wheeling instructions included!

FIVE BALL LOTTO WHEELS - $24.95

PLATINUM LOTTERY/LOTTO™ - $149.95

Prof. Jones Winning Software - (IBM and compatibles only) CD Rom - Windows

The Platinum is the **king** of the Lottery/Lotto software, this **powerhouse strategy** includes all the goodies of the outdated Gold Series **and more**, and is for players **going for the max**!!! Windows-like environment makes software **easy-to-use**. Newly revised and updated to include latest changes and winning strategies, this program is a must for serious lotto and lottery players.

BEAT ANY LOTTO GAME: *Super strategy* features over 20 Dimitrov Systems, hard positional analysis, cluster, bell, % of occurrence, % of frequency, past numbers, two digit numbers, expanded cluster, skip/hit chart, hot number analysis, regression analysis and *unlimited* wheeling systems! Has the built-in goods for 3-ball, 4-ball, 5-ball and 6-ball games and can handle *any number of bets and games* for all states! Now has PowerBall!

The Platinum Series "Plus" Lottery/Lotto™ program allows you to play 3 or 4 number lottery, or any style lotto including bonus or power balls. Play any number of lotteries and lottos, your only limitation is the size of your hard drive.

You aren't limited to playing numbers the program picks. Quickly create your combinations–lucky numbers, or picks from several types of analysis, just 'click' any numbers, and create the wheels.

Entering game data is simple and quick. Type in the numbers manually or use your mouse for the built-in key pad. A couple of minutes a week is all it takes to keep your game files up-to-date.

Regression Testing determines how much game history to use. For example, does using 50 of the previous games give better results than 100? Here, you can see that 54 is the best regression setting since it gives the highest number of 4, 5 and 6-ball hits.

		Testing Best Numbers					
Ball Hits		1	2	3	4	5	6
Regression: 48	Hits:	9	18	8	9	2	0
Regression: 49	Hits:	0	0	0	0	0	0
Regression: 50	Hits:	14	2	0	0	0	0
Regression: 51	Hits:	13	5	6	8	2	0
Regression: 52	Hits:	4	0	0	0	0	0
Regression: 53	Hits:	6	5	2	0	0	0
Regression: 54	Hits:	12	3	7	10	6	4
Regression: 55	Hits:	0	0	0	0	0	0
Regression: 56	Hits:	0	0	0	0	0	0
Regression: 57	Hits:	11	10	1	0	0	0

GREAT KENO PRODUCTS

The Basics of Winning Keno *by J. Edward Allen* In one easy reading, this quick primer teaches you what you need to know about the house odds, the history of keno, the best playing strategies and even the taxes on keno winnings. You'll learn how to make all the bets including straight, split, way, combination, king and special tickets, and how to use them in a coordinated winning strategy. Illustrations and charts clearly illustrate the bets, payoffs, and tickets. Includes a glossary. 64 pages, **$4.95**

Complete Guide to Winning Keno *by David W. Cowles* David Cowles, the world's foremost authority on keno, shows novices everything about keno including powerful winning strategies, honest advice on the odds, and how a player can beat those odds. From a brief history of the game to a thorough explanation of how to prepare every type of keno ticket, to collecting winnings, this book is a treasure house of playing tips, strategies, and anecdotes. Twenty-five chapters present the most thorough and intriguing coverage at keno ever put into print including, for the first time, accurate, computer-analyzed odds charts for every standard keno ticket. 256 pages, **$16.95**

THE GRI MASTER KENO STRATEGY

Finally! David Cowles, the world's foremost keno expert, has released exclusively to Cardoza Publishing, his **powerhouse strategy** on winning money at keno. It is now available **for the first time** and only through us!!!

TIRED OF LOSING? LEARN HOW TO WIN! Learn how to bet the tickets that provide the highest payoffs and push the percentages in your favor, increase winning tickets tenfold using way, combination and king tickets, set goals and plot a winning course, parlay small bankrolls into large fortunes by betting smart instead of haphazardly, and how to stretch your bankroll so you have more winners and chances for big jackpots!

WIN MORE PLAYING KENO! Cowles reveals, for the first time, the magic wager-to-win ratio—a quick way to determine if a keno ticket is playable—plus how to find the most profitable tickets, the real scoop on picking winning numbers, tips from the pros on winning keno tournaments and contest prizes.

THE SECRET TO THE MOST PROFITABLE BETS! Many keno tickets are ripoffs. Learn to avoid the sucker bets and how to slash the casino edge to the bone. You can't change the odds, but you can get the best deals once you learn the secrets revealed here.

FREE ROOM, FOOD & DRINKS? You bet! They're yours for the taking. You just have to know who, how and when to ask—and then how much.

DOUBLE BONUS! With your order, absolutely free, receive two insider bonus essays: *12 Winning Tips From the Pros* the 12 master jewels that can increase winnings drastically, and *The 10 "Don'ts" of Keno*, mistakes made by both novice and experienced players. You'll never make these mistakes again.

Be a winner! Order now, only $50

POWERFUL WINNING POKER SIMULATIONS

A MUST FOR SERIOUS PLAYERS WITH A COMPUTER!

IBM compatible CD ROM Win 95, 98, 2000, NT, ME, XP

These incredible full color poker simulations are the best method to improve your game. Computer opponents play like real players. All games let you set the limits and rake and have fully programmable players, stat tracking, and Hand Analyzer for starting hands. Mlke Caro, the world's foremost poker theoretician says, "Amazing... a steal for under $500... get it, it's great." Includes free phone support. "Smart Advisor" gives expert advice for every play!

1. TURBO TEXAS HOLD'EM FOR WINDOWS - $59.95. Choose which players, and how many (2-10) you want to play, create loose/tight games, and control check-raising, bluffing, position, sensitivity to pot odds, and more! Also, instant replay, pop-up odds, Professional Advisor keeps track of play statistics. Free bonus: Hold'em Hand Analyzer analyzes all 169 pocket hands in detail and their win rates under any conditions you set. Caro says this "hold'em software is the most powerful ever created." Great product!

2. TURBO SEVEN-CARD STUD FOR WINDOWS - $59.95. Create any conditions of play; choose number of players (2-8), bet amounts, fixed or spread limit, bring-in method, tight/loose conditions, position, reaction to board, number of dead cards, and stack deck to create special conditions. Features instant replay. Terrific stat reporting includes analysis of starting cards, 3-D bar charts, and graphs. Play interactively and run high speed simulation to test strategies. Hand Analyzer analyzes starting hands in detail. Wow!

3. TURBO OMAHA HIGH-LOW SPLIT FOR WINDOWS - $59.95. Specify any playing conditions; betting limits, number of raises, blind structures, button position, aggressiveness/passiveness of opponents, number of players (2-10), types of hands dealt, blinds, position, board reaction, and specify flop, turn, and river cards! Choose opponents and use provided point count or create your own. Statistical reporting, instant replay, pop-up odds high speed simulation to test strategies, amazing Hand Analyzer, and much more!

4. TURBO OMAHA HIGH FOR WINDOWS - $59.95. Same features as above, but tailored for Omaha High only. Caro says program is "an electrifying research tool...it can clearly be worth thousands of dollars to any serious player." A must for Omaha High players.

5. TURBO 7 STUD 8 OR BETTER - $59.95. Brand new with all the features you expect from the Wilson Turbo products: the latest artificial intelligence, instant advice and exact odds, play versus 2-7 opponents, enhanced data charts that can be exported or printed, the ability to fold out of turn and immediately go to the next hand, ability to peek at opponents hand, optional warning mode that warns you if a play disagrees with the advisor, and automatic mode that runs up to 50 tests unattended. Tough computer players vary their styles for a great game.

6. TOURNAMENT TEXAS HOLD'EM - $39.95

Set-up for tournament practice and play, this realistic simulation pits you against celebrity look-alikes. Tons of options let you control tournament size with 10 to 300 entrants, select limits, ante, rake, blind structures, freezeouts, number of rebuys and competition level of opponents. Pop-up status report shows how you're doing vs. the competition. Save tournaments in progress to play again later. Additional feature allows quick folds on finished hands.

Order now at 1-800-577-WINS or go online to: www.cardozabooks.com

GRI'S PROFESSIONAL VIDEO POKER STRATEGY
Win Money at Video Poker! With the Odds!

For the **first time,** and for **serious players only,** the GRI **Professional Video Poker** strategy is released so you too can play to win! **You read it right** - this strategy gives you the **mathematical advantage** over the casino and what's more, it's **easy to learn!**

PROFESSIONAL STRATEGY SHOWS YOU HOW TO WIN WITH THE ODDS
This **powerhouse strategy,** played for **big profits** by an **exclusive** circle of **professionals,** people who make their living at the machines, is now made available to you! You too can win - with the odds - and this **winning strategy** shows you how!

HOW TO PLAY FOR A PROFIT
You'll learn the **key factors** to play on a **pro level**: which machines will turn you a profit, break-even and win rates, hands per hour and average win per hour charts, time value, team play and more! You'll also learn big play strategy, alternate jackpot play, high and low jackpot play and key strategies to follow.

WINNING STRATEGIES FOR ALL MACHINES
This **comprehensive, advanced pro package** not only shows you how to win money at the 8-5 progressives, but also, the **winning strategies** for 10s or better, deuces wild, joker's wild, flat-top, progressive and special options features.

BE A WINNER IN JUST ONE DAY
In just one day, after learning our strategy, you will have the skills to **consistently win money** at video poker—with the odds. The beauty is, these strategies are **easy to use** under **practical** casino conditions.

FREE BONUS: PROFESSIONAL PROFIT EXPECTANCY FORMULA ($15 VALUE)
We're including this **free bonus** essay which explains the professional profit expectancy principles of video poker and how they relate to real dollars and cents in your game.

To order send just $50 (plus P & H) by check or money order to:
Cardoza Publishing, P.O. Box 98115, Las Vegas, NV 89193